# Granny's Diaries

Published by
**MELROSE BOOKS**
An Imprint of Melrose Press Limited
St Thomas Place, Ely
Cambridgeshire
CB7 4GG, UK
www.melrosebooks.com

**FIRST EDITION**

Copyright © Ellen Bostock 2006

The Author asserts her moral right to
be identified as the author of this work

Cover designed by Amanda Barrett Creative Design

**ISBN 1 905226 41 1**

All rights reserved. No part of this publication may be reproduced,
stored in a retrieval system, or transmitted, in any form or by any means
electronic, mechanical, photocopying, recording or otherwise,
without the prior permission of the publishers.
This book is sold subject to the condition that it shall not,
by way of trade or otherwise, be lent, re-sold, hired out or
otherwise circulated without the publisher's prior consent
in any form of binding or cover other than that in which
it is published and without a similar condition including this
condition being imposed on the subsequent purchaser.

Printed and bound in Great Britain by:
Bath Press Limited, Lower Bristol Road,
Bath, BA2 3BL, UK

# Contents

PART I BEGINNINGS 1
1 Early Beginnings 3
2 New Arrivals 9
3 Ironstone, Pig Cheer and Privies 11
4 Blue Skies and Buttercups 14
5 Sandshoes and Seaweed 16
6 Brass Bands and Geraniums 21
7 Privy, Earthworms and Bramleys 25
8 Christmas Cheer 32
9 Gone is the Winter 35
10 School Days and Worrying Ways 39

PART II TEENAGE YEARS 47
11 Work Begins 49
12 Visitors, Visits and Dances 54
13 First Kiss 59
14 Goodbye Grandad 62
15 Hard Times 64
16 I'm Not Gladys 66
17 Mystery Man 68
18 The Day War Broke Out 71
19 Early War Years 74
20 Rationing Begins 76
21 Nursing and a Wedding 80
22 Croxton Social Life Peps Up a Bit 83
23 Extended Families 85

PART III The ATS 91
24 Outward Bound 93
25 Rookie Days 97
26 Derby Days 100

| | |
|---|---|
| 27 Goodbye Derby | 104 |
| 28 New Friends | 110 |
| 29 Old Friends and Women Dentists | 114 |
| 30 Bereavement | 118 |
| 31 The Tide Begins To Turn | 122 |
| 32 Homecoming | 129 |
| 33 Civy Street and Monkey Tricks | 137 |
| | |
| PART IV MANOR HOUSE DAYS | 149 |
| 34 Lord of the Ruin | 151 |
| 35 Work and Play | 156 |
| 36 The Music Man | 157 |
| 37 Future Together | 162 |
| 38 Wedding Day | 169 |
| 39 Settling In | 173 |
| 40 1953 | 178 |

# For Granny

Who is always beautiful, and who will never be old enough
to wear purple.
Eternal youth is yours, may your eyes sparkle forever.
All my love, hugs and kisses from,

Ellie X

# Preface

I started writing down my memories of my young days in Croxton whilst we were still living at the Old Manor House in Allington, never thinking that one day I would be living in the old home on Middle Street again. These are purely my own memories: no deep research or other people's opinions. No doubt other people would see things from different angles, but this is how I saw and experienced them. I have called these writings The Tip of the Iceberg because they are only smatterings of my rememberings, the deeper things lying even yet too close to my heart to put into words. So here we go and I hope you won't be too bored.

# Granny's Diaries

## The Tip of the Iceberg

# Part I

## Beginnings

# 1
## Early Beginnings

Like the city in the Bible, our village was 'set on a hill and could not be hid', facing west, the evening sunlight reflecting in the cottage windows setting the whole place aglow like some celestial city. There, of course, the biblical simile ends, Croxton was no more an earthly paradise than any of its surrounding villages in the vale. Within its boundaries there lived and breathed its saints and its sinners as anywhere else on earth.

Croxton looked across a narrow green valley to another green hill, the main road running down through the village from one market town and winding up again to another market town, nine miles away. Thatched stone cottages, one or two later brick ones and a church set on the highest point, parts of it dating from the twelfth century. Large farms and smallholdings supplied the main occupations before the development of the ironstone mines.

Into this environment I was born just before the end of the Great War. My father and mother met when he was stationed in Grantham in the Machine Gun Corps and, after they were married, lived with my Grandad and Granny in a stone cottage in the village. When I was nearly a year old I became very ill and was not expected to survive but, thanks to the local doctor, I'm still here to tell the tale. He performed some sort of operation on me on the kitchen table, opening up my ankles and neck and I still have the scars to prove it. No one has ever told me what the illness was or any details about it, any enquiries I used to make were met with negative answers, in those days nobody talked about such things. However, one old family friend said I lived to break some man's heart or else his pocket; I can honestly say I've never done the latter. For a long time I must have been a sickly child as I didn't walk until I was two, by then Granny Allen had died and my parents continued to live with Grandad in his house rented from the Duke of Rutland. The whole village belonged to him, the villagers going twice a year to the Peacock Inn to pay their rent, 'Muscom Feast' they used to call rent day. About a year after I was born my sister Adelaide arrived. Sadly she only lived a short time, was privately baptised and laid to rest in the churchyard amongst the family graves.

After my father was demobbed he had no job, and having been a townie before the war had to adjust to a life in the country. Across the road from our house was a cobbler's shop and here Dad learned the trade of boot repairer. After the old cobbler died he opened his own business in a little black hut in our yard opposite the back door. Here the people brought their worn out footwear and he would sit in his dusty little shop with its glowing fire in the small iron stove, sewing leather soles onto best shoes, toe caps onto scuffed toes, little patches onto where poor bunions had pressed hard, and straps and buckles onto leggings. Strong soles were fixed onto farm boots with large hob nails and steel heel plates onto heavy ironstone boots. Once a week he travelled round the local villages on his bike, delivering the finished repairs and collecting up the worn footwear: his next week's work. In the summer the shop door stood wide open and, if it was very hot, Dad sat outside on a low chair cobbling away and enjoying the shade of the coal house wall.

Later he became an auxiliary postman, which added a little extra to the housekeeping budget. He wore the post office uniform of navy blue with red piping round the jacket, a red stripe down the outside of his trousers and a coal scuttle shaped hat with his number on the post office badge on the front. He had a heavy red bicycle with a large carrier on the front for the letter bag and parcels, and four times a day he went up and down the hilly road to Knipton, two miles away. Come rain or shine, snow or blow, away he went at seven o' clock in the morning to collect the incoming mail from the post office there, where it had been delivered by van from the main sorting office at Grantham, and brought it back to Croxton Post Office. There, in one of the outhouses, it was sorted out and Dad and Mr. Roberts delivered it, the latter doing the bottom half of the village and Croxton Park and Dad the rest of the village, the Lodges (the outlying farms) and the Grantham side. He finished this about 9 a.m., had his breakfast then took the outgoing mail down to Knipton, then home again till the afternoon. Off he went again at 3.30 p.m. to collect the incoming mail, deliver that round all the village but not the Lodges, then back to Knipton with the outgoing mail, home again and posting was finished for the day. There was a good postal service then, two deliveries and two outgoing mails a day, only a week's holiday in the summer and no bank holidays, except Boxing Day, there was even a delivery on Christmas morning. In between all this he got on with his boot repairing, neither job in any way overpaid.

An aunt and uncle of my mother's kept a grocery shop and post office and, long before Dad became postman, Uncle Tom used to have to meet the mail coach at Harston in his pony and trap. One morning it was noted that Uncle Tom was earlier than usual, when asked why, "Well, Sir," he said, "The pony galloped."

Uncle Tom was a stonemason and woodcarver. His work can be seen in Croxton churchyard and inside the church where there is a plaque on the south wall to his memory. Apart from his shop, there was another grocery shop, a bakehouse with a disused windmill in the field nearby, a butcher, a blacksmith's forge, and a wheelwright. There was also a small sweet shop selling gobstoppers and liquorice bootlaces etc. just opposite the school, all catering for our small community. Travelling salesmen came round the village each week from the local town. In the summer the ice cream man would appear with the ice cream in a container on the front of his bicycle and a penny cornet was a great treat on a hot day. In the winter he was round again, this time with pyklets (pikelets), which we toasted in front of the fire on a long toasting fork, and ate them for tea, soaked in butter.

There was a fruit and vegetable man who brought his wares round on a dray pulled by a patient horse. Mondays brought 'Pick's' van laden with clothing and drapery which you could buy and pay off a little each week until the debt was cleared. On Fridays Pick's hardware van arrived selling everything from matches to dustbins, brooms, clothes lines and paraffin for oil lamps and cooking stoves, everything was brought to the door with a good and willing service.

Eventually a fish and chip van came round once a week bringing an unheard of treat for us. At Friday teatime we would join the crowd round the large window in the side of the van and wait to be served whilst the fat spat and bubbled in the vats and the black smoke poured from the little chimney on the roof. One day, on taking our fish and chips home Mum discovered that I had been given a ha'penny too much change, "You must take it back," she said. "Oh Mum, it's only a ha'penny," I cried, but off I had to go. I felt very embarrassed pushing my way through the crowd and offering up my ha'penny, I felt even more conspicuous when the fish man drew the attention of the people to my honesty. I've never forgotten this incident. Honesty was my mother's great policy, and she used to be fond of quoting: 'It is a sin to steal a pin, to cheat in any way, to waste the time that is not yours, to borrow and not to pay.'

One of my earliest memories is hearing our front door open early on Saturday mornings as I lay in bed, and a voice call out, "Ayer warming yer sen, Uncle?" 'Uncle' was my grandfather who would be sitting by the fire enjoying his first cup of tea of the day, but whether he was really uncle to the man who called this greeting each week I doubt very much, even though in those days nearly everyone in the village was related. Grandad was a foreigner so to speak, a native of a village some miles away, coming to Croxton to work on a farm before he married my Granny. Bob, bow-legged and bewhiskered, was the local carrier. Every Saturday morning he set off for the nearest town in his covered cart laden with goods and baggages to deliver, and with lists of shopping to do for the village people. Often he had passengers too, who sat in a row on each side of the cart. Arriving in town he would put up at the Blue Bull yard, stable Dobbin, and set off about his business in the town with, no doubt, occasional calls at the hostelry for liquid refreshment. On the homeward journey, when approaching the long hill up to Croxton, the passengers would alight and walk up to the top to relieve the weight on the old horse, then get in again and off they would jog home. During the week Bob and Dobbin delivered coal round the village and to other villages in the area, a hard and busy life.

Eventually the people deserted the carrier's cart for a motor van. Dobbin was pensioned off and 'Ayer warming yer sen, Uncle?' became a catch phrase in our house. Grandad said he didn't like these newfangled things and preferred to walk whenever the necessity arose for him to go to town.

The Institute, or 'Stute' as it was called by the locals, was the venue for most of the social occasions in the village. The men and boys had a club there and a large billiard table was installed. Whist drives and dances and the parish meetings were held there.

The Wesleyan Chapel vied with the Church in looking after the spiritual welfare of the people. They used to say that a certain vicar would open his window and call out, "Schism," as the leading lady of the Chapel went by, whether this is really true or not I couldn't say – I do know that when an old lady wanted to take me with her to the Chapel Harvest Festival Mum told me if I went, "I would go up to the moon," but she let me go just the same!

The Peacock Inn stood at the bottom end of the village and was very much forbidden territory to us. Ladies did not go into public houses, and apart from a few female 'characters' it was very much a male preserve. In the yard at the back of the house were stables and tack rooms, and during the hunting season the rich people would stable their horses there and the grooms would stay at the pub. There was a flight of stone steps leading up to a large room called the Club Room over the stables. Here at one time the Club feasts and meetings were held, but in my day the WI held their meetings and social occasions there. I performed in my first speaking part in a play held there when I was at school. I was Snow White and thoroughly enjoyed performing before an audience.

Just down the road from the back gate of the Peacock was a little spring where the people in that part of the village drew their water, a damp, secret, little place built round with stone and kept very clean. Further down the road was the horse pond where the waggoners took their horses to drink after a hard day on the land, a cool refreshing place surrounded by brambles and willowherb, willow trees and tall ashes, a quiet home for moorhens and other small aquatic creatures. Here we found frogspawn which we collected in jars and kept on the school windowsills, and we watched it slowly hatch into tadpoles, but somehow before they actually turned into frogs they disappeared. We would go back to school after a weekend to find the jars empty, we could only think the miracle had happened whilst we'd been away and the frogs had hopped out, but we felt it was more likely the cleaner who had dealt with it, not being able to 'abide frogs'.

From this pond the water ran into the wash dyke, a purpose-built sheep bath, large and square, where the sheep were brought once a year for the dipping. We used to sit on the wall and watch as the men brought their flocks down to the water amidst clouds of dust, baaing sheep and shouting men. The sheep were thrown into the water and doused under it with a good deal of splashing and struggling to be released up the narrow jetty into the field beyond, to shake themselves and dry in the sun, then to be driven away to summer fields and pastures new.

Further still down the road the water poured unceasingly from a tall pipe over a spring, cascading down into a pool at its base, surrounded by watercress and forget-me-nots, and then flowing away under the road to form a lovely stream bubbling its way through the pastures to join the young river Devon, thence to the Trent and on and on to the sea. Here, at the water spout, farmers brought their water carts, large barrels on wheels with a funnel-like opening at the top, to fill up and take back to the farmyards for cattle drinks, and other domestic uses. Village pumps too were the order of the day for the water supply, placed at strategic points in the village. These iron pumps stood encased in their tall wooden boxes, the handle protruding from their sides, and a stone trough to stand the bucket in beneath the outlet spout, paved round with bricks. Here the men would go after work, with their buckets hanging on yokes from their shoulders, and get the supply of household water needed for the next day. They would all congregate and 'village pump politics' and the latest village gossip would be discussed at great length.

We were lucky on our side of the village street. A large tank was installed at a farmyard not far from us and water pumped up to it from a spring down in the fields at the bottom of the village, and piped to a tap in each of our back yards, a great step forward for the few houses it served.

Clubs abounded in the village, a necessity when wages were low and families large, a kind of do-it-yourself insurance scheme. I remember in my earliest years going across to the vicarage with my mother and waiting in the large, dim hall with its ferns and its fish tank, until we were ushered into the study to pay some money into the Clothing Club, saving up for when any members of the family needed new clothes or bedding etc. The men went to another venue to pay into the Coal Club, ready for when the winter fuel needed to be paid for. The Pig Club was also a great insurance when keeping a pig which almost everyone did then, and from which Grandad benefited when his pig died. This would have been a grievous loss had he not been able to collect back from the Pig Club. We also paid into the Nursing Association and the Medical Club. A great help to us when Dad was ill. We were able to have a nurse living in the house and any doctors or medicines were paid for out of the Clubs. Later on, when these had ceased to exist there was the Sick and Dividing Club which Dad paid into. When he became sick so often the small amount paid out each week was gratefully received.

The doctor held a surgery in one of the cottages one day a week coming up from his main surgery at Woolsthorpe. Patients would go in and sit down amongst the antimacassars and aspidistras and wait patiently to be called to his kindly presence. One day Mum had the occasion to take my younger brother Tom to see him. On the way she stopped to chat to someone, letting her attention wander from her son for a while. Shortly after, on being examined by the doctor Tom was asked, "Open your mouth," which he did and lo and behold to Mum's embarrassment it was full of chewed-up hawthorn leaves which Tom had regaled himself with whilst waiting for Mum to stop talking. A doctor from Waltham attended at another house, so we were amply provided with medical attention. A great advantage when GPs dealt with almost everything at their surgeries, only sending people into hospital for the most serious complaints and operations.

# 2

# New Arrivals

Soon after I started school Tom was born. One lovely summer evening mysterious conversations were taking place in the house, I sensed something was about to happen. I felt vaguely disturbed, yet knew not why. Finally, about bedtime Mum told me that I had to spend the night with Aunt Eliza and she would see that I got to school in the morning. I went off with Aunt Eliza to the cottage where she lived as a housekeeper to an elderly man, right on the edge of the village. A great walnut tree by the gate sheltered the house. In the autumn the boys would raid the tree and the old man would chase after them shouting, "Get out of my garden, you lousy thieves." That night I went to bed cosy and warm in Aunt Eliza's big feather bed, and woke next morning with the sun shining through the small window. Aunt Eliza had gone. I suddenly felt lonely and lost, worriedly wondering, "Where was that old man with the beard?" I sat up in bed and looked out of the window and there was my guardian in the garden pulling peas for the midday meal. The fear that she might forget me nagged on, but I needn't have worried. She soon came up and helped me dress, have my breakfast and I was on my way to school. People kept stopping us and I caught a word here and there, "She's got it then, that's good, safe and sound," and "What will this one say?" with sidelong looks at me. I knew there was something special going on but I could not fathom out what it could be. Morning school over, I went home for my lunch and there found out what all the mystery was about. Whilst I was away a new baby had come into the house, "A boy – son and heir," my father told me proudly. Suddenly I felt very abandoned and jealous of this baby who had been brought into the house whilst I was away. Dad tried to get me upstairs to see the new arrival but I would not go, I sat at the bottom of the stairs for a long time just watching my mother's bedroom door. At last I somehow found myself by the side of her bed and there snuggled beside her was my baby brother. I had been an only child until then, now I had to share. Thomas William had come to stay. Two years after Tom was born, Maisie Alma made her appearance, no great upset this time, so I must have accepted her arrival without fuss. Now there were six of us.

# 3

# Ironstone, Pig Cheer and Privies

My grandfather worked on the Ironstone, as the mine was known. He got up very early in the morning and I would hear his boots go clattering down the jitty steps ('jitty' is a local word for the passageway between two houses). He was going to join the rest of the men setting out to their daily work in the opencast mines some way out of the village. They carried their lunches in flat baskets strapped across their shoulders, their trousers tied at the knees with leather straps called yocks. Grandad was a filler, one of the men who, when the blasters had blown the rocks apart with dynamite, heaved the huge pieces into the waiting trucks behind the small engine, which pulled them across country to larger sidings where they were taken on to the steel works. Heavy backbreaking work it was, no mechanical navvies to take the strain. Eventually the huge machines did come and took away the gruelling job of filling the trucks by hand.

When Grandad wasn't working he took me for walks over the countryside, teaching me the names of the wild flowers and where to look for them. We walked in the winter when the snow was thick all around us, branches of the trees creaking under its weight, and watched winter sunsets drop purple shadows across the land, trampling home to log fires and good old English stew and dumplings. In the spring we walked across the hills to woods, the ground beneath covered in bluebells, pink campion, stitchwort, water blobs (similar to marsh marigolds) and the lovely tottering grasses that only seemed to grow in special places.

Every cottage had its vegetable plot and flower garden and many of the men had large allotment gardens on the outskirts of the village. At first Grandad's was one of those up the ramper, or the Grantham road, later these were moved to the lane leading to Little Hill Field. After a hard day's work on the Ironstone he would tramp home, have his dinner then off he would go and put in several hours' work on his allotment. Many hours I have spent there with him too. Some evenings, when the novelty had worn off, Tom and I would huddle by the hedge or the wheelbarrow wishing Grandad would finish and take us home, which he eventually did after cleaning his tools well and making sure that everything was shipshape. He took great pride in his garden and it was a sight to behold, his rows of peas and runner beans all neatly staked. Onions and carrots in weedless, straight rows. Lettuces, radishes, spring onions, greens and cauliflowers in goodly array. Great marrows all stripey yellow and green, a splendid offering at the Harvest Festival. In the autumn it was all hands to the garden for potato picking, Mum and Dad helping to bring the harvest home. Larger potatoes were picked out and these were buried in a large potato pie, as we used to call it. They were piled high in a sheltered corner of the garden and covered in a thick layer of straw, then soil piled round and over them to keep out the frosts and they would stay there until required, safe and warm from the winter weather. The very small ones were kept for pig food. These were boiled in their skins then mashed up with the pig meal and fed to the family pig in the sty to fatten it up for Christmas. Special ones were kept for seed potatoes, later these were set up to sprout on large trays and placed under the beds until growth had started and the time for planting came.

Pig killing was a great event; the local pig-sticker would come to the house on the appointed day, the big copper would have to be filled, with the water raised to boiling point. Amid great squealings the luckless animal would be stabbed in the throat by the butcher, its agonies at an end it was laid out on a low wooden table called a cratch. With boiling water taken from the copper the men would scrape all the hairs off and clean the carcass, then leave it until the next day for the cutting up and the disposing of the body. They used to say the only thing you couldn't use from a pig was its squeal. The bladder was blown up for us and used as a football. The offal, the liver, kidneys and slices of the belly were all taken out and a piece of each put onto plates and 'the pig cheer' was delivered round to friends and neighbours, who did likewise when their turn for the killing came round. The intestines were cleaned out for sausage skins, the meat was put through the mincer, mixed with breadcrumbs and seasoning, and the skins filled to make delicious sausages. Other meat was chopped up to make pork pies. The head itself went to provide brawn or 'collared head', depending on which part of the country you lived in, which was a mixture of meat in a savoury jelly. The feet, or trotters, were well cleaned and boiled, and much liked by the menfolk. The hams and shoulders were cut off and, with the rest of the pig, were laid in a preserving mixture in long boxes and there left to ripen, then removed and hung on hooks on the cottage ceiling, to be cut at through the winter and boiled or fried for breakfast or lunch bag or special occasions.

The old friend who lived opposite used to employ a farmhand to look after the animals. One day he appeared at the kitchen door in 'such a takin'' as they used to say. "Oh dear, missus," he said, "the pig's yetten me lunch, and that's not it, it's yetten me cloth an' all." He seemed more worried about his cloth and what his wife would say than losing his lunch! Needless to say more lunch was found for him and another cloth to take home!

I can just remember Grandad's last pig dying. A sense of disaster hung over the house and a group of men from the Pig Club gathered round the pigsty wall watching its lingering last moments. It so upset Grandad he said, "No more pigs," and the sty remained unoccupied for years. When we grew older Grandad decided to turn it into a playhouse for us. He scrubbed it out and limewashed the walls, painted large birds on them in red ochre, and cut large logs of wood for seats. Many happy hours have we spent there with friends, playing Mums and Dads and hospitals and never realising how lucky we were to have a private little place to play. I always say I started off my housekeeping in a pigsty.

Evidence of another event which took place yearly was a large pit dug in the part of the garden where ashes were thrown. No one spoke much about it, only in hushed tones not meant for little ears. Then one moonlit night, cans of beer were brought up from the Peacock, lanterns were lit and plenty of tobacco brought in. Grandad and Dad dressed in their oldest clothes and puffing hard at their pipes would disappear up the garden, and we would be ushered into the house and the doors firmly shut. Before Grandad and Dad came in again we were in bed, but occasionally a whiff of a not-too-pleasant odour would creep under the door and we could only guess at what was happening. In the morning our guesses would be proved correct as we would observe a large long-handled ladle leaning up against the fence, that the deep pit was all filled in and an unpleasant odour still hung around everything. The annual emptying of the lavatory vault had taken place; an unmentionable necessity in most homes in those days, and one the menfolk did not enjoy!

# 4

## Blue Skies and Buttercups

During our school days Marie used to come every Wednesday to do the weekly wash. A small, cottage loaf figure in a long black skirt and blouse, a large apron, button boots and a squashy black hat sitting comfortably on her grey head firmly anchored with a large hat pin. She would stand in the big whitewashed kitchen almost lost in the steam, which rose from the large copper in the corner where the white linen bubbled and boiled in rich foamy suds. The fire roared away under the copper hole behind the little iron door, and the bubbling and plopping increased and a gorgeous smell of washday pervaded the house. On occasions the whole lot would boil over and a great frothy river flowed out through the back door.

No washing machines then, we had a tall, zinc dolly tub and wooden dolly pegs or a copper ponch (a copper bowl on a long handle) to agitate the clothes to remove the surface dirt. Then the rubbing and the boiling, the final rinsing followed by the blue bath, the wringing out through the large wooden-rollered mangle, and finally pegging them out on the line in the garden at the mercy of the weather, either to blow merrily in the wind and sunshine or hang depressingly limp in the rain. Happily dry they would be brought in, folded, put once again through the mangle, ironed and finally hung up to air on the wooden clothes horse or lines strung across the kitchen above the fireplace.

One wash day I came home from morning school, had my lunch then went up to the kitchen and persuaded Marie to let me blue the handkerchiefs. I got so absorbed in this exciting chore I forgot all about the afternoon school and my parents forgot all about me. When we realised the time, alas, it was long past school time and I, being a very young and new pupil, was terrified that some awful punishment would be meted out to me. "Ne'er mind, wench," Marie comforted me, "you can come home wi' me till they come out a school. They'll not find yer there!" After she had mopped up the kitchen we set off for her little cottage. It was a glorious afternoon, hot and still, the world was a golden haze of buttercups and blue, blue sky.

Marie's cottage was thatched, the eves hung low and the bedroom windows were level with the floor. The door led straight into a dim, cosy room, with rag rugs, large pictures, and china dogs on the mantelpiece. On the low windowsills masses of geraniums splashed bright colours against snowy lace curtains. The fire blazed merrily, making the kettle sing on the hob and a large, black iron pot filled with pig 'tates' hung on a jack hook over the flames, boiling away ready for the pig's tea. These small potatoes boiled in their jackets were delicious to eat skinned and piping hot. Marie would let me take one as she mashed them up to feed to the grunting pig in the sty at the back of the house. I can't remember going home that day, nor my truancy being spoken of again, but I shall always remember Marie and her busy presence.

# 5

## Sandshoes and Seaweed

By the time I was eight the first buses serving the towns and villages were on the roads. Bland's Luxury Coaches and Skinner's Blue Bird were the first ones I remember and later the Silver Queens started a service round the villages to the local towns. Then trips to the seaside were organised by the school and looked forward to with great eagerness and excitement. The Headmaster opened a holiday fund where each Monday our parents could send a little money to save up for their fares etc. All schoolchildren went free, their fares were paid for with money raised by the village people at dances and whist drives during the winter, and we were each given a little spending money. On the great day we had to be up very early in the morning, shivering with cold and excitement in the early chill we would all dress in our summer clothes, sandshoes on our feet, a beret on our heads and navy blazers almost always a necessity on the chilly East Coast. Five big red buses would be drawn up in a line, one behind the other, on the main road and Joe Bland, a tubby little man in shirt sleeves and waistcoat, would be waiting there to greet us in his bluff hearty way. He always drove the first bus. The great excitement of boarding a bus: 'Which one?', 'Where would be the best place to sit?', 'Must be with our friends', 'Must be off', 'Come along there', 'Move down', 'Let me be near the window' were the cries heard in the babble of exhilaration along with a certain amount of pushing and shoving. At last we were all safely aboard, when we were younger we didn't move far from our parents, but when we got older, friends used to try to get together along the back seat.

Away at last, 'Look out Skeggy, here we come', travelling through the morning mists of the countryside and hoping the sun was shining at the seaside. Our first stop was at Boston, right near the Stump itself. Long before we got there we would all be agog to see who would see the Stump first. We all piled out to attend to the wants of nature and buy an ice cream, then back into the bus we all scrambled and off we would go, next stop, the sea, what a long, long journey it seemed. At last there we were, pulling into a huge, sandy bus station, and there was the clock tower, but where was the water? My first sight of the ocean is hard to describe. Our family was walking along the wide pavement all in a row. "There it is," Dad said. I was speechless: in front, seemingly going on and on forever, was a brilliant sparkling mass, no end, no beginning, just eye-dazzling and incomprehensible, a huge expanse of glittering water. Coming up over the road by the clock tower there was the beginning of it all, the waves swishing up on to a huge stretch of sand, lacing and frothing at the edge, then sucking and swirling back again, to advance even further in on the return surge.

I couldn't believe that for a whole day we were going to be here. Off came our shoes and socks, our skirts held tightly above our knees, we gingerly tested the water and we were all splashing and shouting and making the most of this new found pleasure.

We were all given a meal in a large restaurant in the town, and one time coming out of the door, I got separated from my family, blind panic took hold of me, I ran hither and thither screaming my head off, thinking I had lost them forever, but kind hands reached out and held me and a woman from our party soon restored me to my parents. "Always stand still, right where you miss us," my Father said, and I've always remembered that, "No need to go charging about in circles probably getting more and more lost in the process."

Once when Tom was small, he went all dressed up in a sailor suit, navy shorts, a jersey with a square navy collar and a sailor hat, and paddling along the edge of the sea he lost his balance and fell in. What a great upset, "Not a thing you expect a sailor to do," said Dad. Mum always said after that the little suit never really dried out however much she tried, the salt in the seawater always seemingly dissolved again causing perpetual dampness, "And it being the first time he had worn that suit."

After a long day on the beach, paddling, riding the donkeys that plodded patiently up and down, playing cricket, the grown ups regaling themselves with jugs of tea from the tea kiosk on the esplanade, it was time to make our way wearily back to the bus station and start the long journey home. Not before calling at another kiosk to see if the photographs that the street photographer had taken of us on our way down to the beach that morning were ready. There we all were reproduced for posterity on a strip of cardboard. A souvenir of a day at Skegness or as some were wont to call it: Skegsnest. Another stop at one of the many stalls to buy some long sticks of pink rock with

Skegness written right through it from one end to the other, to take home for relatives and friends who had not been able to make the trip. Soon we were all sorted out on our respective buses with our buckets and spades and shells and seaweed, which we were told if we hung it outside the back door would tell us what the weather was going to be like, our rock, and raincoats we'd taken just in case! And all the rest of the paraphernalia one has to take on a day out with children. Spirits began to rise as we pulled out of the bus station in the mellow sunlight of early evening and soon we all started to sing the old popular songs, 'One man went to mow', 'Show me the way to go home', 'Ten green bottles' and so on. Arriving back again in Boston, the usual procedure of spending pennies, some getting fish and chips and quite a lot of men piling into the nearest public house. It seemed

*Maisie and Tom Woods*

*Thatched Cottage and Village*

that we stopped for hours on the way home but it was possibly only half an hour, but once more off we go on the last lap home. More subdued now, quite a few of the youngsters asleep, one or two sick – too much pop and ice cream or a touch of the sun. Sporadic singing would break out as the night mists crept over the flat fen countryside. "Here's Grantham," someone would shout, and then we knew we were nearly home, and the singing would start again.

Someone would take his cap off and go round the bus collecting for the driver and we'd all strike up again with, "For he's a jolly good driver, for he's a jolly good driver, for he's a jolly good driver and so say all of us," and we were back in the darkening main street, a keen wind whipping round us all as we clambered down the bus steps, weary parents carrying sleeping babies, stumbling toddlers and all glad to be home again, a small crowd waiting to help and hear how we had all got on. What a happy, exciting day it had been, a never-to-be-forgotten day, for once again the sea seemed a very long way away, and seaside holidays and day trips in the family car a long way into the future.

The policeman, postman and schoolmaster all lived next door to each other, and just across the road, slightly downhill lived the vicar and his wife, irreverently called John Henry Blossom, after the two early entertainers to be heard on the cat's whisker wireless set. They were a very worthy pair, fairly high Church and genteel and were a great influence on my formative years. Each summer they used to go in their little car to Ely for a 'Clergy Quiet Day' and knowing that Granny Woods lived at Spalding invited Dad to ride with them as far as there, spend the day with Granny and be picked up on the way back. I went too several times. We sat in the 'dicky seat' at the back, well wrapped up against the cool breezes as we bowled along through the flat countryside. It was a great treat as there still weren't many cars about at that time. Dad was one of a family of five brothers and two sisters. Grandad was dead but during his lifetime had been a horse dealer, buying matching pairs and breaking them to harness for the coaches of the gentry in the great days of horse-drawn vehicles. I think most of the family had been brought up with horses. One of Dad's brothers was Uncle Fred, whom I never met. I spent quite a few holidays in Spalding with Aunt Em and Uncle Harry and Cousin Fred in The Millstone, their public house in the town, Grandad went with us. Before we left to catch the bus Mum was tidying up, throwing old bits of paper on the fire and suddenly realised she had thrown some pound notes with them – the bus fare ready for the off on the kitchen table. Panic ensued, Dad managed to rescue the charred remains, no more legal tender. I suspect Grandad came to the rescue because we still managed to set off on the bus and have a lovely, though crowded, holiday in Spalding. Luckily, the pieces of notes rescued from the fire bore the number so, on contacting the Post Office, we finally got the burned ones replaced – a great relief in our fairly poor circumstances.

# 6

# Brass Bands and Geraniums

September brought the Flower Show, held in the field next to the church called the Pinfold. Marquees were erected and here the many exhibits of vegetables, flowers and fruit of infinite variety were arrayed: the culmination of the gardeners' hard working year and great was the competitive spirit. Early in the afternoon the festivities started off with the local brass band parading round the village followed by a straggling procession of people in fancy dress. I was terrified by this great noise and was always glad when it passed our house. Everyone then would tag along behind and follow the band up to the field, where flags fluttered on the ends of the tents and a general air of excitement and anticipation filled the air. Horsemen tent-pegged (a military game), and children ran races, licked ice cream and drank fizzy lemonade from small bottles with a glass marble in the neck. In the tea tent potted meat sandwiches, cakes and cups of tea could be bought, and in the big tent the smell of trampled grass, onions and sweet peas mingled as people pushed around trying to see who had won the coveted red card, and our family were no mean winners. There was the best dressed window competition too, in the morning before the start of the events the judges would walk round the village and choose the winning window. Grandad and Dad entered both our downstairs front windows. They grew beautiful geraniums and pot plants and these were arranged on the deep windowsills in a mass of gorgeous colours with Mum's snowy lace curtains draped behind, a display which often carried off the prize. At last the day would draw to a close; the sun dropped slowly behind the hill and the band would play the National Anthem, all over for another year. People making their way home, some happy and proud, some disappointed, but everyone already looking to next year, and who knows the prize could be theirs.

The next event in the country calendar was the Harvest Festival. A whole weekend of rejoicing and thanksgiving for a harvest safely gathered in. Ladies of the parish decorated the church with flowers and masses of fruit. There were so many sheaves of corn that one stood at the end of each pew. My first job in decorating was to make small sheaves to stand in the windows. The first service was on the Friday evening and the church was full, farmers, labourers, gardeners, housewives and children all joining together in thankfulness and praise. Three services on the Sunday too were all well attended, especially the afternoon one which was a special children's service. Before we went Mum was busy outside in the backyard scrubbing potatoes and carrots, polishing apples from the tree in the garden, and enthusiastically loading we children's baskets up to the brim; far too heavy for us to carry. We had to congregate in the school with our offerings and walk in twos up to the church and I remember the heavy basket banging about against my legs and wishing Mum hadn't been quite so generous. Arriving at the church door we waited for the vicar to come out to meet us, then we all followed him in carrying our baskets right up to the altar, whilst the congregation sang 'Fair waved the golden corn, in Canaan's pleasant land'. At the altar we handed over our 'first fruits' to the vicar, who passed them on to his churchwardens, who piled them on the altar floor, heaps of beautiful fruit, vegetables and flowers, our offerings of thankfulness and love.

When I was older and in the choir we spent weeks before learning and practising an anthem, and the smell of the candles mixed with the scent of the fruit and flowers, the warmth of the church, the fellowship, and the volume of praise stays with me to this day. 'He gives us fruitful seasons, filling our hearts with food, our hearts with food and gladness.' The next day all the produce was taken to the local hospital where it was gratefully received. No National Health Service then to supply all their needs.

November the 5th was the next date, as far as I was concerned, to fear. Fireworks. I was terrified of the bangers; especially the rockets and jumping jacks. The latter, when lit, banged and cracked around on the ground, and the nearer to anyone's legs the greater the fun! Grandad and Dad arranged high stools at the top of the garden to stand the Golden Rains and Fountains on, and the Catherine wheels were pinned to the clothes post, and we and any friends who liked to join in had to stand well back down the garden. I have to confess I spent most of the time in Dad's little shop watching from the window with my ears covered up. I did very warily venture out to hold the sparklers and dance around waving them about like so many demented fireflies! No one was more relieved than I when the last sparks flickered out and everyone trooped indoors to lamplight and a roaring fire. We didn't make a guy but children did come to the door with one, shaking their tins and saying, "Please remember the Fifth November, gunpowder, treason and plot. I see no reason why gunpowder treason should ever be forgot." That to me was a matter of opinion!

After the war the old soldiers banded themselves together all over the country and the British Legion was formed, and Dad was vice-president of our local group. On November 11th, then Armistice Day, was a very close sadness, a day of remembrance for all those who died for

*The War Memorial*

their country in the Great War. There were sixteen men who paid the supreme sacrifice from Croxton. Uncle Tom carved their name on the memorial in the church.

At 11 a.m. on that day all over the country everyone stopped whatever they were doing, men took off their caps as they stood still, and for two minutes a great silence reigned. We all wore poppies sold in aid of the British Legion funds used to help the victims of war. On the Sunday nearest to November 11th there was a special service in church in the evening, the members of the British Legion gathering outside the gates, drawn up in ranks and marching in with their blue and gold banner, their medals clinking proudly on their chests and heads held high. Pride and sadness mingling, their memories all too recent. At the appropriate time Mr Clark, an ex-army officer, moved with the vicar to the marble memorial on the north wall, right in front of our family pew, and hung a wreath of poppies beneath it, then read all sixteen names, finishing off by quoting Laurence Binyon's immortal words, 'They shall not grow old as we that are left grow old, Age shall not weary them nor the years condemn. At the going down of the sun and in the morning, we will remember them,' and back came the sad but firm echo, 'We will remember them'. The stirring notes of the last post and reveille sounded from the back of the church where a trumpeter blew with all his might and sincerity. Finally, the whole congregation sang, 'O Valiant hearts who to your glory came, through dust of conflict and through battle flame'. The standard was retrieved from the altar where it had lain during the service and the men marched out into the murky blackness of the November night.

Some people, of course, who had lost relatives in the war would not join in this remembrance day and would shut themselves away, perhaps a very understandable reaction. But the war to end all wars was over, and the country, one fit for heroes to live in!

# 7

# Privy, Earthworms and Bramleys

Winter came with sharp frosts, often snow and always chilblains. Many were the remedies advised for this painful complaint, including rubbing the feet with raw onion, or snow or even dipping them in the chamber pot. All these I tried, but none worked and I had to put up with sore toes all through the winter. At dusk on short winter days the coal hod was filled, wood brought in and kindling chopped ready for the fire lighting in the morning, and stacked on the hob to dry. The bottoms of the doors were blocked up with sacks to stop the draughts, the hanging oil lamp lit and the fire stoked up. After tea when the washing-up was finished we would all go 'up the yard'. The little red lantern was fetched from the top shelf in the dairy and the candle in it lit from the fire with a long spill. We would all put on our coats and off we would go to the lavatory at the top of the garden. There we would sit in twos on the wooden seat, one small hole for the children and a larger one for the grown-ups. Woe betide anyone who opted out of this routine then decided they had an urgent call when the doors were all bagged up again and everyone settled by the fire. That someone would suffer agonies until an adult would move themselves to accompany them up the yard with all the performance of getting ready for a day's march. I've learned a lot about the moon and stars on these treks and the love life of worms, which would be entwined across the brick path on damp nights. I used to shudder at the thought of treading on them.

Back in the house again Mum would fetch a few apples down from the little room on the stairs called the bacon chamber. I would go with her to hold the candle at a safe distance whilst she filled her apron from the straw in which they nestled to protect them from the winter frosts. They were Bramley Seedlings, cookers, very tart, but we enjoyed them and they were the only apples we ever had except at Christmas.

## Hold the Candle Away

'Hold the candle away from you gel'
My mother would say as we climbed the stair
To the chamber where the apples lay
Spread on the floor on a bed of straw.
She climbed the last steps as I stood by
Holding the guttering candle high
Stooping to choose from the rosy store
Filling her apron with apples galore.
The stars looked down through the small skylight
And winter winds moan round our house of a night
But round the hearth so snug and bright
We sampled the bounty of autumn's warm delight.
Now the apple room's gone and there's no skylight
A larger window lets in the light.
But I often think of mother and I
Climbing the stairs and hearing her tell
'Hold the candle away from you gel.'

*Grace Palin*

The long winter evenings were spent round the table doing our homework helped by Dad who was also quite a good artist and enjoyed using our paint boxes. Grandad took to reading books which I used to get for him from the school library. Mum would do her mending or knit socks on four steel knitting needles. The fire would roar up the chimney and the boiler hum a contented little tune whilst the winds roared around the house or Jack Frost fingered the earth outside transforming everything to a glittering fairyland. Mum and Dad would share the chore of getting supper ready. Then we children would undress by the fire and off we would go to the cold bedrooms. No central heating then and we never had hot water bottles, but if it was very cold Mum would wrap the oven shelf up in an old vest and put it in the bottom of the bed. She would always come upstairs to hear our prayers and tuck us in and her last words were 'Goodnight and God bless you, hope you will have a good night's rest, and waken up well in the morning.'

Friday night was a dreaded night. Syrup of Figs night! We would object strongly to being dosed and would hide under the table and fight and cause a general disturbance. How we hated that syrup. Nevertheless in the end we had to swallow it even if it meant Dad holding our noses to get it down.

On Saturday mornings we had to stay in bed out of the way until Mum had blackleaded the oven and boiler grate. A long job! We would sing hymns and songs to occupy the time and at short intervals shout downstairs, "Can we get up now, Mum?" and Mum would reply, "No, won't be long." At last we were allowed to get up and make the inevitable journey up the yard then wash and breakfast and our friends would be at the back door to see if we were going to play. Out we would go, not being allowed in again until all the Saturday chores were done. That meant all the floors scrubbed. Sometimes Dad would leave his shoe repairing to help. Mum was very proud of her quarry tiles and after they were cleaned would spread out newspapers for us to step on to keep the floors nice for Sunday.

Everything was done on Saturday that could be done to prepare for Sunday. Grandad brought all the vegetables in from the garden needed for the weekend. He shelled the peas or cut the runner beans. How thin he cut them, slivers so delicate you could see through them and how good they tasted at Sunday dinner with roast beef and Yorkshire pudding. After tea on Saturdays old Ned used to come across from the house opposite for Dad to give him a trim and shave. He was a bit simple and walked very stiffly with a stick. Dad used to tease him and I felt sorry for him, but he took it in good part and paid Dad threepence for his pains. After this Dad would take a milk can and go off to the Peacock to fetch Grandad two pints of beer, bring it home, then go back himself until ten o'clock. Grandad would sit by the fire puffing away at his Hearts of Oak, with his beer can on the floor beside his chair and his glass on the mantelpiece and every now and then enjoy long quaffs, leaving froth and bubbles on his well trimmed moustache, and occasionally allowing me a sip – much to Mum's disapproval! Once when Dad was ill Mum and I had to go down to the pub for this Saturday night treat. Not being used to such errands Mum daren't go into this 'dreadful place' so we waited outside until a man we knew came along, and with much giggling got him to bring the can of beer out to us. It never occurred to me to ask why Grandad couldn't fetch his own beer.

Before we went to bed the large tin bath was brought in and filled from the boiler at the side of the fireplace and here we were all scrubbed sweet and clean for Sunday.

We were brought up to respect Sunday as a day of rest from weekday chores and for churchgoing. Mother took most of the morning cooking the roast beef and Yorkshire pudding, using the small oven at the side of the open fire, the vegetables bubbling and boiling in saucepans arranged precariously over the fire and plates laid out along the fender to warm.

After dinner we all went for the usual Sunday walk, a great tradition in those days, only very wet weather keeping us indoors. Sharp, frosty days would see us all muffled up in Sunday best clothes. Mum and Dad, Maisie in the pushchair, Tom hanging on to the handles and me tramping off alongside hoping we wouldn't go too far. "We'll just go as far as the Three Queens," Mum would say, being a onetime coaching inn down a long, lonely lane, where Dick Turpin is supposed to have called – then a farmhouse, or it would be just to the Folly Hole. That was a dump for everyone's old tins and rubbish. A fascinating place to root about in when we got older. Summertime would see us going over the hills amongst the gorse where hundreds of rabbits played and Watership Down hadn't even been thought of! Other families would be out there too and the Sunday promenade was very much part of the social scene.

After tea Mum and Dad went to church and Grandad took over babysitting. Some evenings he would take down ornaments and knick-knacks from the cupboards and tell us all about them. There were one or two very special ones like Darby and Joan. They were a fine china lady and gentleman, arm in arm, and should have been under an umbrella but it had been broken off. There was a pair of blue and white sitting Chinamen, who nodded their heads if you gave them a gentle tap and a really special tiny baby doll called Tommy in the Glass because he always sat in a wineglass in the cupboard.

Grandad would recite very old poems like 'The Sluggard' which went like this:

> Twas the voice of the sluggard,
> I heard him complain,
> You have waked me too soon,
> I must slumber again.
> And the door on its hinges,
> So he on his bed
> Turns his sides and his shoulders
> And great heary head.
>
> A little more sleep,
> And a little more slumber,
> Thus he wastes half his days
> And his hours without number.
> And when he gets up he sits folding his hands,
> Or walks about sauntering or trifling he stands.

> I passed by his garden and saw the wild brier,
> The thorn and the thistle grew broad and higher.
> The clothes that hang on him are turning to rags,
> And his money still wastes,
> Till he starves or he begs.
>
> I paid him a visit still hoping to find.
> He had took better care of improving his mind.
> He told me his dreams,
> Talked of eating and drinking,
> But he scarce reads his bible,
> And never loves thinking.
>
> Said I then to my heart,
> 'Heres a lesson for me',
> That mans a picture of what I might be,
> But thanks to my friends for their care
> In my breeding
> Who taught me betimes to love
> Working and reading.
>
> *Isaac Watts (1647 – 1748)*

Watts was one of the first hymn writers; there was no regular hymn singing in any church before the eighteenth century.

He taught me to sing 'Oh my Grandfather's Clock' and 'All Jolly Fellows that Follow the Plough'. He used to read to us from our storybooks. Our Sunday evenings were happy times.

Soon it was time to go to the dairy and fetch out the vegetables and gravy left over from dinner, and put them in the oven ready for Mum and Dad coming home when we would all eat them for supper with the leftover cold meat – and so to bed.

As we grew older there was Sunday school and later still we joined the choir and Tom became a bell ringer, Sundays were busy days. But we were never allowed to play games or knit or sew. Reading and letter writing were our main occupations. I'm sure we all started off on Monday refreshed and more able to face the week ahead after a Sunday well spent.

When I was ten a few friends and myself joined the choir, our Headmaster was the choir master and the regular organist was called Eric. There were mature ladies and men who were long-standing members, more or less experienced vocalists with varying degrees of ability. They kept their beady eyes on 'us young uns' and woe betide the gigglers and fidgeters during the sermon, nevertheless tricks were played on the unwary.

Our stand-in organist was Florrie, tall and thin who would arrive for the service, cushion under arm for extra comfort on the shiny organ seat. During the hymns she would get carried away with great enthusiasm and press down on the keys and heave slightly off her cushion and, swift as lightning, hands would reach out and the cushion was on the floor and Florrie's anatomy would land on the cold, hard seat. Prominent teeth would bite on upper lip and eyes glare over steel-framed glasses but she never was sure if it was the innocent-looking children standing singing their hearts out who were really the culprits or not!

Our organ blower was our old friend Ned, unfailingly every Sunday he took his place behind the dusty red curtain by the side of the organ and there, hidden from the congregation's view, he solemnly pumped the handle keeping the wind in the pipes when necessary, and when not, hunched on his little seat seemingly napping, but he never missed a cue. If he ever did miss a service one of the boys had to go round behind the curtain and take over the blowing, naughtily, if Florrie was playing he would wait till she was in full spate and let the wind run right out of the pipes and the organ would whimper to a stop. Poor Florrie, she must have suffered but as they used to say 'Boys will be boys'.

Choir practices were one evening a week, when the boy next door popped across the yard to the back door to call for me and we'd climb the hill together and pass through the dimly lit nave of the church to the candlelit choir stalls, and there the choir master put us through our paces for the Sunday services. For festivals and special occasions we practised anthems and our involvement in the church was a natural part of our lives.

At Christmas the choir joined with the Sunday school for a party and received a present off the tree. My disappointment knew no bounds when I was fourteen, I was handed a parcel from the tree and on opening it found it was an apron, and a book mark with 'Do your duty, it is best to leave unto thy God the rest' written on it, a very prophetic present as it turned out. In contrast my friend received a butterfly brooch with pretty glittering stones in it; perhaps someone had deeper insight than I realised or appreciated at the time.

Round about this time the question of confirmation cropped up and my Father and I were candidates. I remember making a conscious though private decision to be a Christian; I felt the challenge to follow Christ and was sure that was the only way. The text of the sermon I heard at the time 'Jesus Christ the same yesterday – the same today and forever' made a great impression on me. "That's it," I thought, "not long, long ago but here and now," and my confirmation was a great occasion for me. We were confirmed at Stathern Church. Dad going in the sidecar of another candidate's motorbike and we girls in the vicar's car.

## The Cow

The friendly cow all red and white
I love with all my heart
She gives me cream with all her might
To eat with apple tart.
She wonders lowing here and there
And yet she can not stray
All in the pleasant open air
Pleasant light of day.
And blown all the winds that pass
And wet with all the showers
She walks amongst the meadow grass
And eats the meadow flowers

*Robert Louis Stevenson*

# 8

## Christmas Cheer

Preparations for Christmas started about the beginning of December when Mother would buy all the ingredients necessary for the mincemeat, plum pudding and Christmas cake. She would wash all the dried fruit thoroughly and spread it out on dishes to dry on the fender in front of the fire and woe betide anyone who picked at it! Her friend Maud always made the cake so enough fruit etc. had to be taken round to her in good time. Mum made all the mincemeat and puddings herself – a large pudding for Christmas Day, a medium one for New Year's Day and a small one for when needed. Each member of the family having a stir and a wish for Christmas, then the mixture was put into the basins with a cloth stitched over the top for a lid and placed in a large oval iron saucepan and boiled over the open fire for hours. Some people boiled theirs in the copper they usually boiled the clothes in. Nearer to Christmas the mince pies were made, pastry to melt in the mouth. Mum always made us a mince pig – an oval-shaped pasty with a snout and currants for eyes. Grandad would buy the large ham to be boiled and cut at during the festive season. He would always have a barrel of beer brought in and placed in the dairy on the old brick block. Tapping of the barrel was a great ceremony with the knocking out of the bung from the bung hole and replacing it with a wooden tap, standing a jug on the floor to catch the drips, and great was the tasting thereof.

At school we made paper chains and Christmas cards and calendars. We sang carols and the Headmaster read Dickens' *Christmas Carol* every year, reading the last chapter on the last day of term.

Our Christmas tree was usually a small holly bush cut from the garden hedge by Grandad and decorated by Dad. It stood in the corner of 'the house', as the living room was then called, on a small black tripod table brought down from the bedroom for the purpose. There it stood in all its glory, covered in tinsel and baubles, sugar mice and real candles which were lit at Christmas teatime. We never took the decorations down then until Candlemass so by February it was brittle and dusty, but at least no pine needles all over the floor. I believed in Santa Claus for a long time because I never could imagine how my parents could afford the presents on Christmas mornings. When I did find out their secret I kept very quiet about it so as not to spoil their fun. Our stockings hanging on the bed rail held all kinds of exciting things. The traditional orange, apple and nuts in the toe, sweets, pencils, painting books and one larger present on the end of the bed. I used to feel with my toes under the covers, hardly daring to breathe in case there was nothing there, then great relief and excitement when I felt the hardness of the parcel and realised 'he'd been'. But we had to wait until morning to see what he had brought. Then Mum and Dad would come in with a lighted candle and in the dim light we would excitedly explore the bulging stockings. Dad being a postman wasn't always there, although cards weren't sent to such a great extent then, letters and parcels were delivered on Christmas Day, only Boxing Day being a holiday, and he was often late getting home. Heavy loads carried on the front carrier of his bike, icy roads, not to mention the odd glass of sherry or a home-made wine at the doors on his round. People were generous with Christmas boxes too; money and occasional cockerels and rabbits were the seasonal cheer. The fire was lit in the parlour and this made it very special indeed, and here we were allowed to have our new toys and books. There were evergreens around all the pictures and paper chains and decorations criss-crossed the ceiling.

When we got older Christmas day started at 7 a.m. with a service in church, so after a quick look through our presents it was out into the cold, dark world where the church on the hill was an oasis of light and warmth. The large round brass candelabra hanging from the roof each holding eight candles shed their bright lights over the Christmas greenery and the festive white altar frontal and shining altar candlesticks. The church would be full and the choir, in freshly laundered surplices, in good voice and the familiar well-loved hymns would soar to the roof and the real Christmas spirit was all about us. The service over, home we would go to a special festive breakfast of cold ham and pork pie, and a closer inspection of our presents. Mum would cook the Christmas dinner of roast chicken and all the trimmings, the home-made plum pudding with luscious white sauce sliding down its sides and a sprig of holly stuck in the top. Dad would arrive home rather later than expected, which didn't somehow please Mum for a while, but after dinner with the washing-up done, we would all congregate in the parlour and the grown-ups would read to us out of our new picture books or we would play snakes and ladders or card games round the fire. Nuts and dates, oranges and apples were set around for those needing to fill up the odd corner until teatime. The short winter day soon ended and the oil lamps lit and the tea laid in the living room, where we would enjoy more cold ham and pork pie, trifle, mince pies and the Christmas cake, all white icing and silver bobbles. Each year a pair of elderly sisters sent us a box of crackers and these we pulled at teatime, out of which came the usual paper hats and novelties, we scrambled for the mottoes and the little pictures from the outside of the crackers which we stuck in scrapbooks. Back again to the parlour for the evening to play with new toys, read and especially to sing hymns and carols until supper and bedtime. Christmas Day over, Boxing Day was more relaxed, but still festive, and though we had one or two Christmases when Dad was very ill, or just recovering from an illness, when funds were very low, our parents still managed to give us a very special time.

Soon after Christmas Day came the Sunday school treat when we all went off down to school dressed in our Sunday best with our china cups and saucers, plates and spoons – to eat the jelly with. There was a tall tree that almost reached the ceiling aglitter with tinsel and baubles and lighted candles and a small present for everyone. After tea we played the usual party games of Blind Man's Buff, Spin the Trencher, and In and Out the Windows. Then it was time to hand out the prizes for attendance and lessons over the past year. These were always books with our names written on a special label on the flyleaf. Each child then received a present from the tree, an orange and a bun to take home.

Though we didn't have parties of our own we were invited to quite a few. I remember feeling very shy at first but usually ended up enjoying myself. Once I won the prize for pulling the ugliest face, never a great effort on my part I used to think.

New Year's Eve came always a bit sadly, I thought, the passing of the old year. But the bells pealed out a welcome to the new at midnight. Men making their way home from the Peacock raucously singing carols and generally whooping it up would cause Mum to turn down the wick in the oil lamp – a precaution against bangs and shouts at the window had the revellers realised anyone was still up. After this it was back to school and life took on its normal pattern, secure and uncomplicated it seemed then as though things would go on the same forever.

# 9

# Gone is the Winter

Gradually spring came with the awakening earth, with the first snowdrops and aconites, the planting and the sowing, the chicks and the woolly lambs. Then long Lent, as it seemed to us, when we all tried our best to give up sweets until Easter, which Mum always managed to do right to the end of her life. Even on Mothering Sunday, which is also called Refreshment Sunday when one is allowed to break the fast for the day, she never would and carried on until Easter with her self-imposed denial. Lovely Easter with its special services, chocolate eggs and possibly new shoes or a new hat, the old folks saying if you didn't wear something new the birds would mess on you! As the daffodils and wallflowers bloomed in the gardens, and the blossom burst out in the hedgerows, came May Day.

The first of May was always a special school holiday, traditionally to welcome the longer warmer days, and each village around had its own May Queen and celebrations. In Croxton it was strictly a girls-only day, the boys being warned the day before in school not to follow the procession round the village or make a nuisance of themselves. Only the under-fives were invited to the tea in the afternoon. The evening before we went all round the village begging flowers from the cottage gardens, which in most cases were willingly and freely given. Only one or two cantankerous people sent us away with a flea in our ears and there was always an anxious discussion who would best be the ones to knock on these doors. We would end up with a glorious array of flowers all standing in buckets in the schoolroom for the night. Next morning the older girls would get up early and meet with one or two adults there and trim the garland, a wet, cold job, but well worth the shivers in the end. The garland would either be a doll sitting in a small chair or two hoops fitted inside each other to form a sphere, whichever was the fancy of the day. The flowers all bunched up and tied on the whole arrangement would be a mass of spring flowers surmounted by a large umbrella lily. A pole was then fixed through the centre so that it could be lifted up and carried round the village by two of the bigger girls.

The Queen was always the oldest girl in the school and she and her maids of honour would all wear white dresses and veils on their heads held in place by a wreath of fresh flowers. All the rest of the younger girls, her subjects, would follow on behind also in white dresses but no veils. We would form a procession at the school about nine o'clock in the morning and start off round the village calling at every house singing our May Day songs and receiving a few pennies in our collecting box. Sad to say May mornings always seemed to start off cold and wet and, to our great disappointment, usually we had to wear coats over our white dresses.

Our first song was 'Gone is the winter, gone is the snow' and we'd often sing this with the rain pouring down and our fingers blue with cold. However, mostly as the day wore on the sun would come out and we would discard our coats and sally forth like butterflies emerging from chrysalises in our finery. By lunchtime the village round was finished, the little ones tired and glad to be home again, but the older ones, after a snack, would be off to the Lodges and Croxton Park. This time we would leave the garland behind and set off through the fields, first arriving at Croxton Lodge about two miles out of the village. Here we were given a great welcome and taken into the front garden and regaled with lemonade and biscuits, and were glad of a rest under the large cedar tree, which is still there today.

Then off we'd go again along the old coach road to Croxton Park singing round the houses by the fish ponds where monks once caught their food, and near to a site where it is said certain organs of King John's body are buried. We would visit the Ironstone where the men, mostly fathers, grandfathers and uncles were working and they would generously drop coins into our boxes with a great deal of chaffing and good humour. Wearily we would make our way home, slightly bedraggled and definitely footsore, but after a rest we would all meet up again at the school where the village ladies had prepared a sumptuous tea of potted meat sandwiches, cakes, tea trifles and jellies. At the end of the meal the Queen would make her speech, mostly a shy, hesitant thank you to everyone, then we would summon up enough energy to play the traditional games of Nuts in May, Oranges and Lemons, and the Farmer wants a Wife, and whilst we were thus engaged the ladies would count the money from our box. This would be shared out amongst us, the smaller ones getting the least and the Queen a little extra. At last the day was over and home we would go, weary and slightly worn. The Queen and the older girls would have left school by next year, but a new Queen would be there with her maids of honour and they would be off again following in the footsteps of their mothers and grandmothers before them.

## May Day Songs

See the day the welcome day is dawning
Cloudless the sky this happy May Day morning
Wake now wake the group you must be joining
And on the green to dance this bright May Day

Hark the pipe and table gay resounding
On village green our dancers tripping merrily
Eyes are sparkling rosy cheeks are blushing
Happy are we who get this bright May Day.

Gone is the winter
Gone is the snow
Now to the forest gaily we go
This is the day we all love to sing
Come forth join our band and merry be

*Grace, Tom and Maisie Woods*

> Come let us tread our measure
> And seize the spring time pleasure
> This is the day we all love to sing
> Come forth join our band and merry be.

Another date we used to keep in May was Oak Apple Day, to commemorate King Charles hiding in the oak tree. The 29th used to see us all going off to school with a sprig of oak leaves pinned to our chests. The day before, Grandad would have been out getting a small branch from a nearby oak tree and leaving it in the soft water butt overnight to keep it fresh. If we forgot to wear it on the next day the boys would sting us with nettles up to 12 noon, but after that they couldn't touch you. Before I left school the custom had died out, but if it did nothing else it did make us remember one particular date in history.

A little ditty we used to say was:

> 29th May Royal Oak Day
> If you don't give us a holiday
> We'll all run away.

# 10

## School Days and Worrying Ways

The school wasn't very far from our house, a little way along the village then down the school lane. Three children used to call for me, to see that I got there safely and Mum used to stand on the front steps and wave to us as we rounded the corner. Violet, Olive and Joan were gamekeeper's children and had to walk a long way through the fields to reach the village, as did all the children who lived at the outlying Lodges and farmhouses. All would bring their lunches with them, and either go to relatives or friends to eat, or stay at school, in the winter sitting round the large tortoise stove, or picnicking in the playground in the summer.

Boys and girls played in separate playgrounds and entered the school by separate doors, though we were all taught in the same class together. When we had a games period we all joined together and played either rounders or cricket or did physical jerks. Even in the winter we were made to go outside at playtime regardless of the weather. On the coldest days we huddled in the little back porch, packed like sardines in a tin. If you were big and strong you pushed your way to the back wall where it was warmest but the younger and not so pushy shivered by the door. I suffered agonies from chilblains, and being trampled on gave me great pain and misery. In the summer, forms were carried outside and we did our lessons under the shade of the large walnut tree, which grew in the stack yard next door. Drowsy afternoons with the cooing of wood pigeons and buzzing of insects amongst the leaves overhead. Later on in the autumn ripe walnuts dropped off the tree but we were not allowed to eat them, it was the cane for anyone with the telltale brown stain on their fingers.

My teacher was Miss Prowse, whose father had taught my mother. She was a fifty-sixth cousin, twice removed, as Grandad used to say, a relative through marriage on my mother's side. Miss Prowse taught us to read by hanging a very large oiled cloth picture book over the blackboard and, picking out the words with a wooden knitting needle, she would intone 'A cat sat on the mat'. And woe betide anyone who didn't pay attention, the wooden knitting needle would beat a sharp tattoo on unwary knuckles. When I moved out of the Infants Room into the Big Room my teacher was Miss Daft, an unfortunate name for a school mistress but I can never remember it being used as a joke against her, I don't think we ever gave it a thought. She lived with her mother in rooms in the village and both were very kind people as I was to find out much later in life.

We were thoroughly taught the catechism at school and at ten years old went to a special service in church to be catechised, that is, we had to repeat the catechism from 'What is Thy Name' through the 'Commandments' to the 'Duties to God and our Neighbours', we were then presented with a small bible from the Hallam Charity. Later when we were fourteen we had to know the second half of the catechism, the 'Desire' and the 'Sacraments', then we received our 'big bible', a larger printed one, presumably for when we grew old and our sight wasn't so good! There were many bibles in our house dating from my Great-grandfather's of 1836.

My next move at school was to the Top End of the Big Room into the Headmaster's class. My seat for a while was right next to the School Attendance Board where each day the number of scholars attending school was written up. The highest I remember was 110 children on the register. Everyone stayed at school then until they were fourteen or won a scholarship to the local grammar school at eleven. With the Headmaster we started to study for this exam. I would dearly have loved to pass the ASE, the Annual Schools Exam, as it was called then, but just at that time life took on a very worrying turn at home and left me thinking that they wouldn't be able to send me to grammar school even with a scholarship. Dad was taken seriously ill with pneumonia, this so affected his lungs that it was the start of ill health for the rest of his life. We had a nurse living with us during the day at first, going out to sleep at our friends' houses at night when Mum would take over sickroom duties. After a bad crisis in the middle of the night when Mum had to run through the village to knock up the nurse for help, it was decided that Tom and I would go up to spend the nights at Mr and Mrs Derby's little thatched cottage on the main road and the nurse would have my bed. Mum carried on bravely; long worrying days keeping family life going on as normally as possible; long anxious nights sitting beside Dad's bed. The house always tidy and the smell of disinfectant hanging over everything. All around had to be kept very quiet. Children were asked not to throw their balls up at the house walls, as they were wont to do when playing in the street, as the bumping heard inside the house disturbed the invalid. No antibiotics then to clear up infection quickly, healing came slowly and with long, patient nursing.

One day, coming in from school I saw a yellow basin on the table with savoury-looking brown stuff sticking to its sides, "Ah," I thought, " potted meat", running my finger round the bowl and licking with gusto. "Yuck, whatever was it?" whilst I was spluttering away Mum came in and informed me that it was the remains of a linseed poultice nurse had just made to put on Dad's chest! That taught me to look before I licked! Linseed poultices or no, Dad had to be taken to hospital for further treatment and a further long worrying time ensued.

Poor Tom had a nasty boil on his face at this time and nurse insisted on bathing it but Tom thought otherwise and shut himself in the sideboard cupboard, to no avail, nurse spotted him and bathed and squeezed his little cheek until she said she had 'removed the core'. The usual treatment for boils and abscesses in those days.

We took our written exam at Branston School, two miles away, almost a foreign country to we children then. The Headmaster walked with us through the fields and lanes and we nervously sat and pondered and worried and tried to do our best. I did not feel really unduly bothered, my mind was on a see-saw wondering which would be the best, to pass or not to pass.

Later we went to Branston again for the oral part of the exam. After the first part I was sent to sit at the back of the room, whilst the others read and did other tests but I was never called and I thought they had forgotten about me. I was too nervous to enquire and just went home with the rest feeling that somehow I had missed out on an important occasion. It wasn't really a surprise to me that I only came through with an A3 grade instead of an A1. I think Dad couldn't understand it and had a few well-chosen words with the Headmaster much to my embarrassment. Mum didn't mind, she had the idea I might have been educated above my station and 'never be the same girl again!' So I carried on at Croxton school monitoring, library keeping and sitting in with the lower classes when teachers were away and this I thoroughly enjoyed.

As soon as we were old enough to be sent out on errands by ourselves, we went up the lane to a little farm each morning before school to fetch the day's supply of milk. The farmer's wife ladled it straight out of the pails into our cans all frothy and warm from the cows. We had a favourite trick on the way home to see if we could swing our can round and round like the sails of a windmill without spilling any of the milk. We got very adept at this but Mum would scold and say it turned the milk sour. If we needed extra we had to go up again in the evening for more, an unwelcome chore when we wanted to get out to play. Another little errand I used to do after school each day was to go to the village shop to buy four packets of Robins for a couple of farming brothers who lived in the lane with their mother. I would get tuppence (two pennies) a day for my trouble plus the fag cards from the cigarette packets. This was a great help to me as we played a game very popular at the time of 'flicking the card'. Someone flicked a card and everyone else had to flick their cards and try to cover it, if they did the one to cover the cards won the lot. "Got any fag cards, Mister?" was a regular enquiry to cigarette smokers around.

In the spring as the days lengthened it was time to start the traditional games and the street was full of children with skipping ropes, wooden hoops or trundles, as we used to call old bicycle wheels with a long piece of strong wire fastened to the hub which we would trundle about with us. Whips and tops were a great favourite – peg tops and window breakers were whipped up and down the street with great enthusiasm. We drew rings round the flat top with coloured chalk so that as it spun it created pretty patterns. Sometimes the spike would come out of the top and then the owner nipped up to Dad's shop and he would put a new hobnail in and the top would go spinning off as good as new. What a great playground the street was with only the occasional farm cart and hay wagon to momentarily stop their play. Racing round 'the tabes' was another year-round favourite. The tabes were the houses and gardens which comprised a complete block with roads round them and one child would set off one way round the tabes and another go the other way and the race was on to see who would get back to base first. Fox and Hounds too was a good game. The whole village became the hunting ground. The fox went off to hide and the hounds would follow, the leader calling all the time 'Whoop your hollow or my little dogs won't follow' and the fox would call 'cooee' or give out a long howl and so point the direction in which to start looking for him. At dusk of an autumn evening the four corners of the village would be filled with the 'whoops' and 'hollows' of foxes and hounds alike being called in for supper and bed.

Our garden ran in a steady incline up to the top hovel, once the cowsheds, the lavatory and what we called the top yard. On the left hand side Dad had his beautiful herbaceous border, a strip of grass then the old brick path and on the right hand side a wider strip of vegetable garden separated from next door by a hawthorn and holly hedge. In the middle of this patch was the Bramley apple tree, and at the top by the lavatory hedge another supposedly eating apple tree, though the fruit was hard and always tasteless, planted there more to aid privacy with the tall hedge which hid the door of the loo. Up the middle of all this, on the edge of the brick path, the clothes line ran from the top of the yard to the bottom, fixed at intervals to three tall posts. It was the bottom one of these posts that was my strength and stay in times of trouble. The others were bought ones, tall and square with pegs through their tops to wind the clothes line round, but the bottom one was a smoother round one lightly covered in grey lichen and smooth moss, a relic from some old building. Domestic upsets, quarrels, worries or frights I would be out there with my arms tightly round it, my head resting against its hardness. Here I, being very thin, felt that I could melt into the post and not be seen, here I could see down into the house, or hear when quarrels had subsided. If I felt ill and didn't want to admit it I would cling shivering to its unyielding strength. When Dad had words with my Headmaster over my not passing the scholarship exam I clung to my post until the Headmaster had gone on his way and the front door closed and Dad was back in the house. I hardly dare leave my support to go in and find out the result of that confrontation. However, I never did find out what was really said then, but I know Dad felt better for having said it!

There always seemed to be the boy next door to play with and I grew up rather taking boys for granted; it took me a long time to realise that at some stage boys stopped being good pals and that there was a serious side to the boy and girl relationship. I was devastated when the last boy moved out of the police house and went to live some miles away. I clung to my comfort post in the garden, but nobody guessed how lonely I felt without him. The next policeman who came, though very good neighbours, had a much younger family and by this time I was a grown up working girl.

Our church was dedicated to St John the Baptist so the week nearest to St John the Baptist's Day was feast week. Before my time there were bands and marching of different guilds, feast suppers and great shenanigans when according to a very old lady literally all the men were drunk most of the time. She told the tale of herself, her sister and her mother sitting crying at home every bit of the day of the supper knowing that her Father would come home the worse for drink and be very violent towards them. However, by my young days things had settled down somewhat, bands and marchings and boozy suppers were a thing of the past. Now the fair came, with its great traction engines driving the roundabouts, its swing boats, its shooting gallery, fortune tellers, coconut shies and all the paraphernalia of the fairground. They took over Hallam's Field across from North Stall field, and for three days the village echoed to the ranting music of the merry-go-round, the shouts of the barkers, the squeals and shouts of the youths as they pulled higher and higher in the swing boats, or crashed headlong down the helter-skelter. I liked the roundabouts best, the swings made me sick, and I always felt suspicious of the hard-faced, hard-voiced show people. Not having a lot of money to spare for such frivolities we were taken round once, and I was never sorry that I was never allowed to go again. Tom would congregate with the smaller fry of the village as the fair arrived and would hang around 'helping' to set up the amusements and side shows. His house is now where the shooting gallery used to stand, and he says he is still digging up the clay pipes, which used to be the target for the marksmen. Feast days over the fair people would dismantle everything, pack up and move off to the next venue and Croxton would settle down once more.

So the growing-up years and school days rolled past. By the time I was taking my ASE Tom was only just starting school and Maisie was only three, so there was a lot of difference in the time and development between us.

Nothing was ever said about the job I would do when I left school. Grandad would sometimes tease me and say I'd be skivvying, which upset me greatly, but I felt the inevitability of it and railed against it as my fourteenth birthday drew near. At last it arrived and at Christmas I sadly left school, shed my knee-high socks for long black stockings

*Grandad Allen, Mum, Tom and Maisie.*

which I hated and faced adolescence with reluctance and trepidation.

Whilst I was at school there had been talk of sending all the over-elevens to Bottesford School but it had never materialised. However, by the time Tom was eleven it had come to pass and he was amongst the first to be bussed there and back each day and the village schools, as I had known them, were never the same again. This also marked the beginning of the end of the close-knit village community, old ties and old traditions loosening and horizons widening. Motor vehicles became numerous, tractors began taking over the carthorse jobs on the farms, and aeroplanes became a common sight throbbing across the sky. Silent films gave way to 'talkies', glamorous film stars became the gods and goddesses of youth, and big picture palaces were the in places of entertainment. Radio had passed the cat's whisker stage, and the trade in accumulators for the wireless set was big business, entertainment, news and views were brought into the home from far beyond the village boundaries, and I was looking for my first job.

### Croxton Lodge Circa 1940

A distant village on a hill
Windows golden in the setting sun,
A cuckoo in the nearby trees,
The scent of hayfields on a gentle breeze,
These I remember from when I was young
As we strolled in the garden when the day was done.

The rumble of wagons homeward bound,
The plod of the horses over dusty ground,
The voices of men as they made their way
Towards stables and home after a hot, busy day.
Long lingering shadows over the grass,
These I remember as the years pass.

A tall, grey-haired lady with work-worn hands
Still for a while from domestic demands,
As we walked together on the dewy lawn
And spoke quiet words, of which deeds are born,
The essence of peace and goodness still
Stays with me now, and always will.

*Grace Palin.*

Great it is to believe the dream

# Part II

## Teenage Years

# 11

# Work Begins

The farmhouse kitchen was warm and cosy on that bright, spring evening in early May 1933. A glowing fire in the bright range, large willow pattern dishes on shelves around the walls, Windsor chairs and an old grandfather clock ticking majestically away in the background. My mother had brought me down to Croxton Lodge for an interview for the job of daily help. I was utterly miserable, absolutely and for sure I did not want a skivvying job. I was fourteen and had left school at Christmas with the hope that I would be able to work in a bookshop, pens and paper were my first love and my secret ambition had been to become a writer. Now with each tick of the old clock that ambition was fading further and further away.

Before she married, my mother had been a nursemaid to Mrs Shipman's two children who were now grown up and introduced to me as Master Billy and Miss Molly. As was agreed wages were small, five shillings a week, but mother said that didn't matter as I would learn to be a good housewife, it seemed to be the be-all and end-all of a woman's life at that time.

"She will need two morning dresses and a black dress, the white aprons for afternoons, house shoes, working aprons and a harding apron for floor scrubbing." Mrs Shipman was cataloguing my wardrobe, I shuddered inside, but now I had to bow to the inevitable with as much grace as I could muster. We walked home through the darkening fields, a journey I was to make for the next nine years. My mother was satisfied and pleased that I had found a good place near home, and with the Shipman family of whom she was very fond. I who had never done a stroke of housework in my life, my mother always saying, "You'll always have enough to do when you leave school," was wondering how I was going to cope. The biggest worry of all, was how was my pride going to cope with my skivvying job. It was to take many falls in future years, but I never could rid myself of my besetting sin. The intervening days before starting work were taken up with getting my necessary clothes ready. Apart from the house dresses etc., I had a good strong mackintosh and sou'wester and wellingtons to stand me in good stead when the weather was at its worst. At last the day for starting my job on the farm arrived, Mum saw me off from the front steps, and stood waving as I walked off down the hill and round Vicarage Corner, carrying my aprons and house shoes in a brown carrier bag. At first I walked there and back, but by July Granddad had bought me a new Halford Club bicycle, of which I was very proud and which was a great leg saver. My way was down Cripple Alley, I never did know why they called it this, unless because it was so rough it crippled you if you didn't take care, nobody seemed to know. However, later it became known as Chapel Lane for down there hidden behind a farmhouse was the Wesleyan Chapel. Then out into the fields and on to the old coach roads, which were in use when coaches travelled between Belvoir Castle and Croxton Park. Now overgrown with grass, shepherd's purse and dandelions, they were a favourite walk for the village people on Sunday afternoons. The young river Devon which started from a spring somewhere in Croxton Park ran through the valley, here chattering and sparkling over its shallow bed of stones or there flowing silently between steep banks covered in wild forget-me-nots, campions, stitchwort and meadowsweet in their due seasons.

Here I was at 7.30 a.m. on a spring morning reporting for work as a daily maid, and here was kindly Mrs Shipman waiting for me with my first task. I put on my new apron and went with her to the back kitchen where the messier chores were done. Eggs washed and packed ready for collection on Fridays, when the egg man would call and take them to the egg packing station in the next village, where they would be graded into their various sizes, then distributed to market outlets in the surrounding towns. Here too, vegetables were prepared, rabbits skinned, poultry dressed, boots cleaned, laundry washed and a hundred and one other tasks pertaining to a busy life on a farm.

Under Mrs. Shipman's instructions I carried a bucketful of boiling soda water out across the drive to the milk place where the milk buckets were waiting to be scrubbed, and my practical education started forthwith. The cows had been turned out into the fields long since and the cowman, nicknamed 'Docker', had gone home for his breakfast. He had already swilled out the buckets with cold water, now I had to scald everything and scrub them out with a long-handled brush, going well round the 'ears' and handles, making short work of any germs lurking in forbidden places. After all this the buckets were once again rinsed out in cold water and turned upside down on the scrubbed pine table. The floor swilled out and everything left spick and span in readiness for afternoon milking. After which this process was repeated once again, for a while, my last chore before going home at six o'clock. In the morning this chore done, it was time for breakfast. Master Billy came in from the farm and Miss Molly from her poultry feeding and we all sat down to breakfast in the kitchen, they at the middle table and I at the side table, an arrangement which surprised and dismayed me, but I began to realise this was the order of things and I had to accept it.

After breakfast the dishes were washed, the vegetables prepared and the eggs washed. In the winter there were oil lamps of varying shapes and sizes, which had to be trimmed. There was the large hanging lamp in the dining room, brass table lamps and small lamps with handles which were carried around the house. All had to be replenished with paraffin, the wicks trimmed to make sure they were level with no sharp points which when lit would cause black smoke on the shining glass chimneys. These had to be cleaned and polished and all left ready for lighting when daylight faded. I soon learned the routine and settled down more or less to life at Croxton Lodge. Each day of the week had its own particular jobs to be done. One day was bedroom-cleaning day, no labour-saving devices then. There was a vacuum cleaner, an archaic contraption; it had a long metal suction pipe joined to a metal cylinder at the top of which were small bellows, then the handle. One held the handle with one hand whilst the other pumped away at the bellows and so sucked up the dust into a small bag inside the cylinder. This was quite hard work and I was more encouraged to use the old method of sweeping carpets. Newspapers were soaked in a bowl of water then wrung out, torn up and scattered all over the carpet, then down on hands and knees with a stiff hand brush. I would sweep the damp bits of paper towards the door, thus the dust stuck to the paper and was prevented from flying all over the room. On one bedroom wall, I remember, were two pieces I learned as I did the chores, the prayer 'Shades lengthen, the evening comes', and another little piece about rest being the 'fitting of life to its sphere'. Rest was not easily come by in the busy life on the farm; there was always some job to be done. However, I was allowed ten minutes' sit-down in the afternoon, before more household chores, or later on, in the winter, before going out to feed the poultry.

Bread making day would find Mrs. Shipman on her knees on the hearth, a large panchion (an earthenware bowl) in front of her, kneading away at the dough. Pushing and pulling and thumping, her face red from her exertions and the heat of the fire, wisps of grey hair in disarray round her flour-smudged face. Having brought the dough to its right consistency she would settle it in the panchion and with a deft flick of a knife make a cut in the top, place a heavy blanket over it to keep out the draughts then it would be placed on the rack over the range to prove. Later when it had risen to almost twice its original size there would be more thumping and kneading, little bread rolls would be formed and larger loaves; the whole lot left in their tins to prove a little longer then into the oven it would all go. What a wonderful smell would pervade the kitchen as the baking went on. Sometimes Mrs Shipman would kindly give me a loaf to take home to my mother, which was greatly appreciated.

The first things I remember making were rock buns, nutty flip and a chocolate sandwich cake, Mrs Shipman herself doing the pastry. She brought me a thick, stiff-covered exercise book in which she encouraged me to write down any recipes I took a fancy to, and over the years I have added more.

Friday was kitchen cleaning day and, in my first weeks there, I would arrive in the morning and Mrs Shipman would be hard at work cleaning the big cooking range. All moveable parts would have been lifted off, plate rack, oven door, flue door, etc., and laid on newspapers on the kitchen floor. It was my job to clean and polish these. Blacklead and elbow grease were the order of the day. The edges of the doors and hobs were steel and these were burnished with steel wool until they shone like silver. The tap on the side of the boiler was brass so that had its own polish. Mrs Shipman would sweep the soot from the flues of the chimney as far as she could reach and scrape the ashes from under the oven and boiler, and blacklead the carcass and polish it until you could see your face in it. Then the whole lot would be put together again, the fire lit and reflecting in the shining surfaces, a sight to behold. When I had learnt how to perform this Friday morning ritual the whole job was left to me, hard work, but great satisfaction in a job well done.

After this the kitchen floor had to be scrubbed; hot soda water and Vim to get the worn flags white. "Not too big a breed," Mrs Shipman, would say, as I reached as far as I could with cloth and scrubbing brush, "A little at a time or you will leave tide marks." So I scrubbed and there would be the floor all shining white, and along would come someone with rubber heels and there were black marks ground into the whiteness again. What a thankless task housekeeping seemed to be.

My Grandfather, now retired from his job on the Ironstone, came down to the farm to do the vegetable garden and odd-jobbing. I well remembered the love and pride in his eyes when he saw me scrubbing a floor. I knew he was thinking, "What a little woman I was." I felt utterly trapped in domesticity and wept tears of self-pity into the bucket. Then I would think that God had put me there for some good reason and I would love and serve as best I could.

One day Grandad was helping to put the turnips through the turnip cutter for the animal feed. The roots were fed into the top of the machine; someone turned the handle of the great wheel, which rotated the knives inside. Grandad must have been careless and got his fingers caught, and the knives chopped his finger-end off with the turnips. Nothing much could be done for him at the farm, so it was off to the doctor's surgery. I was allowed to go home with him to make sure he was alright. First we had to walk through the fields and then Grandad set off by himself to walk the four miles to Woolsthorpe to Dr Hudson's surgery. There his finger was dressed and he walked back home again; a tough old gentleman was Grandad.

## 12

## Visitors, Visits and Dances

Mrs Shipman had become a widow during the time my Mother had worked there. All through the years she had worked very hard to keep the farm going; now she was taking in paying guests to supplement the income from the land.

The first to take up residence for a while was a governess who, during the week, turned the drawing room into a schoolroom and received five children of local gentry for private education. These young ladies arrived each morning in their chauffeur-driven cars and disappeared through the front gate, into the house via the front door, and I wouldn't see much more of them. Sometimes they would play croquet on the lawn and in the afternoon they would go home again, whisked away to nurseries and nannies, and a life beyond my ken. Soon the need for them to be there ended and life returned to normal. Later another family and their nanny came each year for the hunting season, making a great deal of extra work. Riding boots were added to the farm boots, leggings and assorted shoes I had to clean in the back kitchen.

One morning, I remember, the two boys not much younger than myself playing soldiers outside the kitchen window whilst waiting to go off for a day's shooting. "Left, right, left, right," their young voices rang out on the frosty air, as they smartly smacked their guns to their shoulders and marched up and down. Alas, the war wasn't far away and a few years later brought the real thing to the boys and one was very badly wounded.

In the summer two elderly ladies were guests for a while. Coming from the city they enjoyed the peace and quiet of the country and didn't move very far out during their stay. Sometimes I had to put on my dreaded black dress and white apron and wait on them at luncheon. Once one of them watching me whilst I laid the table said, "Grace, you have lovely hands, it's a treat to watch you use them." I shyly accepted the compliment, but wondered at it, as floor scrubbing and vegetable preparation were not exactly beauty treatment. I learned later that they would have liked me for their maid, but I was too young, I shuddered at the thought, would I never rid myself of my serving image?

After I had been at the farm for a year or two Miss Molly went away to Agricultural College to learn about poultry farming, so helping to look after her hens and ducks was added to my tasks.

On arriving at the farm in the mornings I would lean my bike against the ivy-covered wall of the house and enter by the back kitchen door. There I would change into a yard coat and out I would go to feed the feathered family. The food was stored and prepared in the meal place next to the chicken yard, just across the drive. In the morning the birds would have wet mash, this was mixed in a large tar barrel cut into half lengthwise. First the water was put in then scoops of meal added and the whole lot mixed together with a spade to the required texture, quite a muscle-developing job. This would be loaded into buckets, carried round to the hungry flock, and shaken into their long troughs; the pop hole opened up and out would come the greedy mob. A living tide of flying feathers, loud squawkings and every bird for itself. The ducks, a bit more cumbersome, but no less greedy, would flutter, flap and squawk and paddle great flat feet into their troughs; a most unmannerly lot. Some of the hens were out in the fields which meant that I could put a bucket of food on each handlebar of my bike and do a meals on wheels service round the huts, a great leg saver, though rather bumpy. In the afternoon the same rounds again but this time there would be grain in the buckets, and the eggs would be collected.

On spring mornings after the free-range birds had been attended to it was the turn of the broody hens to be fed and watered. These birds would all be sitting on duck eggs in a long row of nest boxes in the paddock. The procedure was to lift them off, gently tether them by one leg to a stake in the ground and place the food and water by them. Then give them a short spell to eat, stretch their legs and attend to the wants of nature. After they were all satisfied they were put back on their eggs in the nest boxes, the lids put back on and they would settle down to another long, patient wait. Eventually the day of hatching would arrive and there they were, tiny yellow bundles of fluff cheeping away under 'Mum's' proudly fluffing feathers. When all were hatched out some would be loaded into special cardboard boxes and transported to customers as day-old ducklings. Others would be kept to send away as week-olds, or whatever age the customer would require.

I remember once there was a terrible thunderstorm, rain bucketing down from a dark, angry sky, water running in torrents off the buildings and causing a river to flow through the farmyard. Going out to the chicken yard to feed afterwards I found, to my distress, lots of little dead ducklings, all drowned, their small bodies lying cold and stiff beneath the dripping lilacs. Oh, why hadn't they had the sense to shelter when the storm began?

Before the busy haymaking time I had to take my annual holiday. Very often I would spend the week with my friend in Nottingham who lived there with her aunt and uncle. Sometimes I would just have a lazy time at home enjoying the rest and freedom from chores. One summer day there was a knock at our front door and there on the steps stood a man with a new brightly striped deckchair balanced beside him. "Miss Woods?" he said. "Yes," I said wonderingly. "I've been asked to deliver this to you," he replied with a twinkle in his eye. I thanked him and took the chair unbelievingly from him, I read the label, 'From Mrs Shipman' it said. She had ordered it to be sent to me so that I could relax in the garden during my holiday, a very kind and thoughtful gesture and very much appreciated.

One holiday I'd arranged to go with my friend to stay with her aunt in the Lake District and I looked forward to it very much. However, the weather turned very hot early and the hay was ready for making, would I please postpone my holiday? Of course I did and went to work as usual. Dad was rather cross and said testily, "Grace, when are you going to start living for yourself," I didn't really know what he meant.

The summer days were long and busy. I had to be at work by 7.15 a.m. and got home later in the evenings. There was soft fruit to pick from the garden, gooseberries, red and black currants, raspberries and strawberries to be turned into jam and jellies. Some bottled in Kilner jars tightly sealed, larder shelves filling up with goodies for the winter months. Beans to be sliced and put into large jars between layers of salt, eggs to be put down in isinglass to preserve them for when eggs were scarce or more expensive.

The poultry was let out earlier in the mornings and fed later in the evenings and, when all the daily tasks were completed, I would go bumping my way down the pig field on my trusty bike and on to the old coach road. The evening filled with the scent of new-mown hay and syringa blossom, the voices of the men in the hay fields and the rumble of wagons going home to the stack yards drawn by strong, willing horses. Cuckoos calling from deep in the woods, rabbits sitting outside their burrows or nibbling the short grass as the shadows lengthened, pheasants feeding in quiet places, and the windows of the village on the hill reflecting the golden light of the setting sun.

At one point in my journey the road dipped down towards a gate through tall oaks and thorn bushes bordering the banks of the stream, which at this point ran under the road. In the summer it was cool, welcome shade. The stream sparkling in at one side of the road, coming out deep and green and almost still on the other, where midges danced over the water and insects buzzed in the trees overhead. On winter mornings the trees would be all aglitter turned to a fairy world by the sharp frost or weighted down by heavy snows. A great hush of all things sleeping would cover the great white world, only the stream would be laughing as it plunged heedlessly under the road, sparkling as ever in the pale winter sunlight. Winter nights were altogether a different kettle of fish, riding home on my bike, mostly not showing a light in case of prowlers or poachers, I would approach this piece of road with just the slightest tremor of fear. It would be dark under the trees and the stream didn't seem to be laughing any more, just hurrying under the road and being swallowed up in the depths of dark, silent water on the other side. Sometimes a stoat would squeal or a fox bark somewhere in the unseen woods and I was glad when I had passed through the gate and turned into more open country towards the lights of home. Before I could reach that desired haven I had to climb the hill. In the mornings I would whiz down its bumpy track on my sturdy bike, not even stopping at the gates but riding alongside them, leaning over, opening them, going through and closing them again in a matter of seconds. But homeward journeys were different. Being too steep to ride up, I would alight at the bottom of the hill and leaning heavily on my bike I would push up to the top, lost in a dream world. Often I would plan stories to write when I had time, but mostly I never got round to putting them down on paper. By the time I reached the last gate I was back to reality and on my last lap home.

It wasn't all hard work and sleep. There were lots of whist drives, dances and socials. Dances started at 8 p.m., but before that there was a spell in a cold bedroom getting dressed up by candlelight. Mother waged war on vanity; we had always been discouraged against looking in mirrors and personal adornment, so we didn't think too much about these things. I hadn't a great opinion of myself in form or face, however it was a pleasant surprise on looking into a convenient mirror in the farmhouse kitchen to see that I wasn't too bad. Skinny with a big nose, a pudding basin haircut, à la papa, natural colouring and good teeth. I managed to get by unadorned. For the dances I would sometimes put metal curlers or pipe cleaners in my hair for a bit of a curl, but this was an uncomfortable procedure to go to bed with, so I didn't bother very often.

We all wore long dresses for the dances and I well remember the excitement when Mum and Dad bought me my first dance dress, turquoise taffeta, and silver dance shoes. All dressed up and ready to go, my friends would call for me and off we went down to the Stute where a local band tuned up, and we took our places on the side of the dance floor, expectantly eyeing the young men on the other side, secretly hoping we wouldn't be wallflowers. As the music warmed up and inhibitions fell away one by one the boys invited us to dance and the evening was happily in full swing. Ballroom dancing was the thing. Foxtrots, quicksteps and waltzes and the inevitable Paul Jones, where the ladies made a ring on the inside whilst the boys circled the outside, and when the music stopped your opposite number claimed you for his partner. The boy who asked you for the last dance escorted you home and, more often than not, after that joined his mates and walked quite a few miles home to the next village. No alcoholic drinks were allowed on Stute premises, but just after 10 p.m., when the Peacock had closed, a noisier element would arrive and stand just inside the door. The village policeman would put in an appearance and keep a good-humoured though beady eye on proceedings. There was no violence, just merriment and the occasional ribald shouting. Nothing ever got out of hand of which I was aware. One particular young man who had joined the air force used to invite me to dance the Old Time Waltz with him. "Hold tight!" he would say, "I'll fly you around the corners," and off we whirled, my feet hardly touching the floor. Sadly he was killed during the war on a bombing mission over Germany.

# 13

# First Kiss

There would come a morning when there was a nip in the air and a mellowness in the noonday sunshine. A quietness of one season taking over from another and autumn would steal into our busy world. The stack yards were full of hay and cornstacks neatly thatched against the weather. On the stubble the hens and ducks would roam for miles gleaning the grain the harvesters had left behind. Apples, plums and damsons hanging ripe on the trees in the orchard, a sumptuous feast for wasps and flies. Swallows congregated on telephone wires preparing for their long journey to warmer lands, the cuckoo gone long ago. The smell of bonfires in the air and apple logs burning on the evening fires indoors.

In the early mornings I would meet the huntsman exercising his pack of foxhounds ready for the hunting season. Scarlet coats shining bright in the morning sunlight, their charges running hither and thither making dark trails in the long grass as they rudely brushed off the sparkling dewdrops eager to find some familiar scent. Only once did I meet a fox. He stood in the middle of the road watching me as I sped towards him. I thought he wasn't going to move out of my way, but as I got closer he turned and unconcernedly trotted away across the field, no doubt to his lair in the nearby woods. The gentry came to their country houses or hunting boxes as they were called, employing grooms and stable boys to look after their horses. These grooms, like the huntsmen, would be out exercising their mounts, getting them in trim for the season. One of these men, called Paddy, whom I used to meet regularly on my way to work, took a liking to me and would deliberately wait for me at the bottom of the hill, mostly riding one horse and leading another, sitting easily in the saddle and well in control of his restive mounts. We would ride side by side as far as the farm, and if truth be told, I in mortal fear of being trampled on by those clattering hooves. Eventually he asked me to meet him after work one evening, my first real date. We met on the familiar hill, he loomed out of the darkness and slipped an arm around me and before I realised what was happening he drew me to him, his head came down and blotted out the stars. I felt as though I was being suffocated as his lips pressed onto mine. "I'm being kissed!" I thought, "For the first time!" "Not for the first time," he said, and I in my sudden adult awareness kept my own counsel. Not for me to give him the satisfaction of knowing that I hadn't been kissed before. We met quite often and went to the village dances together, and to Grantham for the cinema where there were four picture houses to choose from and the glamour of the silver screen was in its heyday.

Boyfriends came and went. I had a good idea of the kind of man I wanted to marry and wanted to do more with my life other than settle down to eternal domesticity, that was not my style. I was still bent on having other fish to fry, though how I was going to achieve anything other than the daily round and common task I had no idea. Periodically I would have a restless time when I would really want to get away to a more challenging kind of life and I would tell my parents furiously that I would only stay for another year. But love and duty bound me tightly and I had no idea how to break the bonds.

Autumn would bring a special visitor to the farm. A beautiful big shire stallion would arrive, clopping majestically up the drive, its mane and tail dressed in coloured ribbons and led by a tall, thin, wizened man in a yard coat and leggings, a flat cap on his head and a cigarette in the corner of his mouth. He would lead his charge round into the farmyard amidst great whinnyings of excitement from the waiting mares. On these visits the groom would come into the back kitchen to eat his sandwiches and I would take him a steaming cup of tea or sometimes a bowl of soup. The smell he brought in with him of sweating horseflesh was too nauseating for words, I used to think.

Later the threshing machine came with a great deal of huffing and puffing and the stack yard was a humming hive of activity and dust. It was all hands on deck for the men: some on the stack throwing the sheaves down to the drum; men on the drum pushing them into the machine, where the grain was threshed out and came pouring out into the sacks at the back; the man waiting there pulled it away and heaving it on to his back carried it to the barn. The waste, or pulses, was also poured out onto the ground under the machine and a man would be kept busy pulling this away, and all the time the humming and throbbing filled the air. As the work went on, the rats and mice in the stack would flee for their lives and men with sticks and dogs would be standing around to catch them as they ran out. When all was finished and the grain stored away in hessian sacks in the barn, the threshing machine and its team would pack up and move off to the next farm awaiting their services. Once again the stack yard would be peaceful, the haunt of hens and starlings and the ever-watchful cats. Cattle were brought into the crew yards for the winter and the carthorses would plod home to their stables at dusk, filing into their places with a clink and a rattle of chains. The waggoner would groom them down and supply them with hay. They would munch contentedly there whilst the mists of the back end of the year crept closer to the garden hedge. The farm workers then went home to their lamp-lit cottages to a welcome hot meal and a quiet evening with the newspaper or the wireless.

# 14

## Goodbye Grandad

In March, when I was seventeen, my dear Grandad caught a chill and took to his bed for the first time in his life. He had been a fine strong man on the Ironstone, a great gardener, a man who loved the countryside and, to the last, had carried great branches of trees home over the hills for winter fuel. Never wearing a topcoat or hat he was finally brought down. I felt great sadness, they let me go upstairs to see him. Two old ladies sat with him and I lost my tongue. "Say something to him," they said, but all I could do was to sit on his bed and put my hand on his arm. He turned to look at me and said, "My hair's white now, isn't it gal?" I squeezed his arm and whispered, "Yes," and crept away. It was the last time I was to see him alive. My mother and father sat with him through the night. When I woke in the morning a weird, unearthly sound came to my ears. Grandad was singing 'Rock of Ages' in his hoarse old voice. All through that old hymn he sang, 'Wash me Saviour, or I die.' Cold hands clutched my heart. I knew his three score years and ten were long passed and he was resigned to his fate.

I managed to get off to work at the farm, but was allowed home early to discover that Grandad had been taken to hospital with pneumonia and there wasn't much hope. My mother and father went off to the hospital, prepared to stay the night, and I was left in charge of the house, and Tom and Maisie. With the help and company of the boy next door and my friend Hetty I managed to get through the evening. We all sat on the fence at the top of the yard chatting, but our hearts were very heavy. We all loved Grandad. The sun went down and it was time to get the young ones in and prepared for bed, there was a knock at the front door and there stood the vicar's wife to tell me there had been a phone call from Dad. Grandad had passed away and they would soon be home. It was over. Now I must get a warm fire and a meal ready for when they came home. The first loss in the family that I had to face and I didn't go to work again until after the funeral.

They brought Grandad home and he lay in state in the parlour, looking very much like Grandad but so still and peaceful. The house was dark with all the blinds drawn. Neighbours came in with hushed voices to pay their last respects to Tom Allen and look in on him for the last time.

The day of the funeral was a bright, blustery day. The undertakers and bearers arrived at the front door with a hand-drawn bier. Four good friends of Grandad were to pull him up the hill to church and lower him to his last resting place. In the top kitchen on the scrubbed, round oak table bottles of beer and glasses had been laid out for them, as was the custom, whilst the mourners gathered together in the living room preparing themselves for the long walk up behind the coffin to church. At last they carried Grandad out of the front door for the last time. The coffin placed gently and silently on the bier and floral tributes placed on and around it, and two by two we formed a slow, black procession through the village, the passing bell tolling mournfully every step of the way. They laid Grandad beside Granny by the north-east corner of the church where the bleak winds whip round off the hills and the morning sun first touches the tombstones.

# 15

# Hard Times

After Grandad died Dad took over the tenancy of the house and the empty chair on the opposite side of the hearth. His chest problem was always with us, once again in early winter of 1936 he was admitted to hospital, and this time he needed an operation. My mother used to cycle to Grantham on visiting days and sometimes I would go with her. Not being used to a lot of traffic we weren't very keen on riding through the town, but 'needs must when the devil drives'. One day just after the traffic lights had been erected by the Angel Hotel we arrived at the crossroads as the lights changed to red. Mother charged across. "If she's going, I'm going," I thought and pedalled furiously after her, to the irate shouts of a policeman. We had to laugh about it afterwards but the consequences could have been serious. Looking back I think it was our sense of humour that helped us through our very worrying times. Eventually Dad slowly pulled through his illness and was allowed home, and gradually things returned to normal.

During this year the story of King Edward VIII's involvement with the divorced American, Mrs Simpson, broke and he decided he would rather give up his throne than live without her, and the abdication followed. As Prince of Wales he and his brothers were often in this area, hunting with the Belvoir or the Quorn, and what stories the locals would have to tell about them. Edward and Mrs Simpson were banished to France where they married. It seemed a sad end for the uncrowned King of England, Great Britain and our Empire beyond the seas. His brother, the Duke of York, next in line became, as historians have put it, an unwilling King and May 1937 saw his coronation. Croxton put out the flags and buntings, flying St George's flag from the pole on top of the church tower. Tea parties were held and mugs with his and Queen Elizabeth's picture on them were given to the school children. Once again there was a family living in Buckingham

Palace. Princesses Elizabeth and Margaret making up the foursome and a well-balanced family they proved to be.

My sister Maisie was now eleven years old and sadly she developed sugar diabetes. We were all very upset and worried. Sugar, sweets and cakes were denied her and she was committed to three injections of insulin a day which mother learned bravely to give her. It was the start of long spells in hospital having diet and insulin balanced and continuing with her schooling as much as she possibly could, being very brave and sensible about it. Visiting at the hospital was only allowed one evening a week for an hour, and an hour and a half on Saturdays and Sundays, so letters travelled frequently between home and hospital to cheer the patient up. Still not many convenient buses on the road on Sundays, so once again Mum had to get on her bike, this time accompanied by Dad, and start the hospital visiting all over again. Sometimes they would cycle down to Knipton and catch a more convenient bus from there. On one of these occasions Mum had the misfortune to lose control of her machine and shoot over the handlebars into a bunch of nettles at the side of the road. This painful situation was alleviated somewhat by the comic figure of a passer-by who peered down at Mum anxiously, saying, "Ayer ut yer?" Mum, never slow at seeing the funny side of things, had to laugh and 'Ayer ut yer?' became another of our family catchphrases.

# 16

## I'm Not Gladys

Life went busily on as usual at the farm. Tom and Maisie attended Bottesford School, Tom was getting on towards leaving age, and ugly rumours of war were creeping into our lives. Large numbers of territorial soldiers came for their summer camp to Croxton Park and carried out their manoeuvres round the countryside in more ways then one. The Women's Royal Voluntary Service was founded to help in all kinds of ways during a crisis. They set up soup kitchens, canteens and hostels for service people and to go wherever help was needed. I joined this service and, although issued with a badge, was never called on to serve. The Auxiliary Territorial Service was founded and women were trained to take over some of the duties performed by men in the Army to release them for service at the front. Air Raid Precaution duties were imposed on local councils, groups were formed to deal with casualties during air raids, and air raid wardens were appointed to enforce the blackout regulations and generally be in charge. I joined the ARP and attended lectures on gas detection and how to deal with gas casualties. I attended First Aid and Home Nursing lectures given by the Red Cross, passing my exams so well that the queen bee of the Red Cross and the Matron of Grantham Hospital tried to persuade me to go in for nursing full time. They seemed to think I was just the type of girl they were looking for. However, I strenuously refused to be bulldozed into anything until I was really sure what I wanted to do. No point in jumping out of the frying pan into the fire. Civilian gas masks were issued to everyone. The ARP people had to be on hand at the school to instruct everyone how to put them on and make sure they fitted properly and how to test for gas. The masks were carried in little brown cardboard boxes. Dad wrote our names on ours in bold black letters so that we could see them clearly in an emergency. G. Woods sprang boldly to the eye on mine and many were the 'humorous' remarks made by strange young men. "Hello Gladys. How's Gladys?" being the most popular. I hated it. People made pretty covers for their boxes, but soon the shops were selling canvas or imitation leather cases with a long strap to wear over the shoulder. This made them more convenient to carry as for a while we had to take them everywhere with us.

In April 1939 the first men were called up into the forces. The Prime Minister, Mr Chamberlain, was going back and forth to the continent with his policy of appeasement. War was almost upon us.

# 17

## Mystery Man

In June I went for my holiday to Nottingham to stay with my friend Betty. The first evening I was there, Betty's firm's staff dance was being held at the Palais de Dance and I was to go with her, a real treat for me. I arrived in Nottingham later than expected and her aunt met me off the bus. Betty had already gone to the dance, I was to join her there. As soon as I had changed into my dance dress Aunt C. kindly took me to the dance hall and then left me to find my own way in. This didn't prove too difficult. I found the cloakroom and then made my way rather nervously to the edge of the dance floor. Gorgeous, foot-tapping music and couples swaying together in swishing rhythm. A great, swirling glass ball glittering in a myriad of light suspended from the ceiling and a fountain playing in the middle of the floor. A great galaxy of colour, noise and movement. "How on earth was I to find Betty in this lot?" I wondered and felt very vulnerable all by myself in this huge place. I needn't have worried. Betty and her friends had chosen a table on the edge of the floor quite near the door so that they would see me as soon as I arrived. They soon drew me into their crowd, and to my surprise I was invited to dance almost straight away. This was the opening to the great evening, a new experience for me. Village dances with the local boys in their Sunday best had been my norm till now. Tonight I was being swept onto the dance floor by young men in dinner jackets and I felt at one with the city ladies in their lovely dresses. We danced around the floor to the strains of Billy Cotton's Band, the glittering ball flashing and the fountains played and sparkled. The evening was magic.

These few days with Betty were spent window-shopping in the daytime and talking half the night away as we shared a bed in Aunt C.'s little back room, the Westminster clock downstairs chiming away each quarter through the night. Sunday came, the end of a happy weekend, or not quite the end. The best was yet to come.

Betty went with me to the bus station to see me off. As we stood talking I became aware of two ladies talking to an air force boy. Our eyes met. It seemed as though we had already known each other. The bus came in and I decided to get in and claim my seat for the journey home. As I stowed away my case the airman also got in and placed his case on the seat beside me with a smile, then got out again to talk to the two ladies who turned out to be his aunts. Time to go. In he got and put his case up on the rack and sat down beside me. The bus moved off and we leaned to the windows to wave our last goodbyes to our respective companions. In no time at all we were in conversation and bells rang and blue birds sang. The ticket inspector got on and proceeded to inspect people's tickets. Where was mine? I wasn't sure. Who cared about the tickets anyway? My companion helped in the search, turning my handbag upside down and spilling everything out, and there it was. The inspector satisfied, we returned to our conversation. Amongst the things in my handbag was a piece of paper on which I had been practising typing my name and other things. We had a brief discussion on this and there we were at Grantham, what a quick journey that had seemed.

He reached for both of our cases and we mutually agreed it would be a good idea if we put them in the left luggage office and went for a walk by the river, until our respective buses were due to take us on the last lap of our journey home. He to Cranwell, where it turned out that he was an officer cadet, and I in the opposite direction to Croxton. No thought was given to the parting that was to come. By now there was a light shower of rain which wet the lilacs overhanging an old brick wall and spilled their nostalgic scent on the summer air. We walked hand in hand and talked and lost all account of time. Suddenly by his watch we had to turn back to the bus station again. We stopped by a lamppost. He drew me to him, sweet, clean and fresh and said quietly, "May I kiss you?" Gently our lips met. The world had changed in that space of time and life would never be the same again. The sound of buses revving up brought us to our senses and there was the red, double-decker Midland bus slowly drawing away from the Leicester platform. Panic! I mustn't miss it, the next one was far too late. He caught my hand and we fled towards it. "Get in," he said, "Stop it whilst I get your case." I leapt onto the step as he rushed up with my case and thrust it into my hand. He ran alongside the bus, but it was gathering speed. I stood on the steps till we rounded the corner. My last sight was of him standing there a lone figure on a near-empty bus station, I was sailing away into the sunset and we didn't even know each other's names. Somehow I was so sure we would meet again, it was meant to be. How had we been so foolishly absorbed not to bother about names? Why hadn't I stayed till the next bus, even though his would have gone out long before mine? Other boys retreated into the shadows, no one else would do. He had mentioned that his cousin worked in the Co-op offices and they had almost gone to the staff dance on the evening Betty and I were there, but had decided against it. Betty checked round the offices, but so many people worked there that without knowing his name there wasn't a hope of finding out anything about him. Time passed and still no word from him. I was hoping he would remember our names and addresses, which had been tipped out of my handbag on the bus, but it was a forlorn hope. I was blind to all other young men and dates were refused as I waited for my blonde, blue-eyed airman. I was so sure he would find me.

# 18

## The Day War Broke Out

September 3rd was a bright, mellow autumn day. As usual at morning service in church my friends and I were there in the choir, and a sparse congregation sat in the knave. As the service was almost drawing to its close there was a tense pause as the door clicked open, and the lone dumpy figure of the Headmistress of the school entered, making as much haste as her short legs and the hallowed ground allowed without being unseemly. We had just reached the end of a hymn, and still stood watching wonderingly as this solemn lady approached the vicar waiting for her at the altar rails. She arrived there breathless but managed to convey her message, leaning over and whispering long and earnestly into his ear, then having accomplished her mission she plodded to her pew. And we waited all agog to hear what had transpired. The vicar cleared his throat and raising his voice, he declared, "I have to tell you," etc., etc., "and as from 11 a.m. today this country is at war with Germany." My friend beside me sank to the seat in tears, "What's the matter?" I asked. "Bob will have to go," was her reply. Bob was her brother and had just about left school. He's not old enough, I thought. For myself the tiniest bit of excitement fluttered in my breast. This was soon suppressed and replaced by a great wonder of what would happen next, actually the thing that did happen next was that we all sang the 'National Anthem' with great fervour. "Let us pray," exhorted the vicar, and we knelt in the peace and silence of our familiar surroundings, and prayed for a happy deliverance from this catastrophe that had been thrust upon us.

Out we went into the sunshine, nothing had changed, everything looked normal, apples hung ripe on the trees, swallows gathered on wires, housewives cooked dinners, the war seemed a long way away, and anyway it wouldn't last long. It didn't seem as though it would make any difference to our family. Dad had done his bit in the Great

War and was too old to be called up now, and Tom was still at school; we had no idea how long and hard the conflict was to be.

The complete blackout of all buildings was enforced in case of enemy aircraft coming over at night, the blackout curtaining was on sale and Mum and Dad put up black blinds at all the windows, and painted the edge of steps and kerbs white so that they showed up a little in the darkness. Croxton hadn't any street lighting then, but the lights in all the towns went out, railway carriages and bus windows were painted over, and small blue bolts replaced the regular lights. Sign posts and station names were removed, and the church bells were forbidden to ring unless an invasion occurred. So the country went into what was called the phony war, nothing really happened to disturb the peace of the countryside.

October 22nd was my twenty-first birthday. Nobody had big parties now that there was a war on we had to be careful with food and provisions, nevertheless Mum and Dad did arrange a little get-together of my close friends, I even had an iced cake with a silver key on it. Gene, Hetty, Betty, Mavis and Nora gathered together in the parlour to toast me in sherry and offer their presents. I had one or two handbags and a pen, Hetty gave me a cake stand and Betty a green glass dressing table set, Mum and Dad a hair brush and mirror set and the Shipmans a watch.

Now I had reached the age of discretion there was still no sight or sound of my airman, but still hope beat in my breast. Soon after my party a strange thing happened, a note was pushed under the door, the message read: 'Dear Grace, meet me at the Banks 7.30 L.S.' No more, no less, who on earth could it be? I thought who ever it is can get lost; I'm not walking down to Banks Wood on a dark night to meet some unknown person, so I ignored the invitation. Several more notes arrived but I still ignored them. Then I started to get curious, one had actually come under the door when Dad was in the passage, he had hurriedly opened the door but not a soul was in sight. Right, I thought when the next one came. 'Meet me at the Church 7.30', this I will do. On the appointed evening I collected a torch and set off up the hill. The wind was rustling the leaves in the gutters and a searchlight silently swept the sky overhead. It was a bit creepy, we'd all been thinking the notes were a hoax and I wasn't convinced that anyone would be there, however, I went quickly and quietly round the corners, shone my torch discreetly around, but no shape loomed up out of the shadows, I felt a wee bit disappointed. Back home I went feeling a bit flat, only to find another note under the door saying: 'Sorry Grace, urgent recall, leaving 7.15 love L.S.' If it was really someone trying to contact me, why didn't he put his name? I came to the conclusion it was someone having a laugh at my expense. Then a letter arrived from L.S. saying he was sorry we hadn't been able to meet, as he had been staying at East Poole with some friends on sick leave, he had had his car down and had hoped we could have a good time. It was signed: 'love Leonard. P.S. next time don't be so fussy.' Parents and friends kept their eyes and ears open just in case any clue cropped up about the mysterious stranger, none ever did, but I got one last letter, saying that he was leaving for France the day after I received it, and that's the last I ever heard of Leonard S. Had it been my blonde airman of Nottingham? That was the nagging thought on my mind. Long after, Betty sent me a cutting from a Nottingham newspaper with an account of the death of a Mr Severn of the Co-op office staff. It recalled the fact that his only son Leonard had been killed on a mission with the RAF. Well, whether it was a hoax or not, that was that and gradually it was all pushed to the back of my mind and other dates began to take over.

Tom left school and was immediately taken on by Jack Wildman, decorator, joiner and undertaker, who had taken over his grandfather's business up by the church. He made farm gates and sheep troughs etc., went out measuring up the dead and making coffins. He himself being dumped into one and the lid put on, a sort of baptism into the trade. He went out with Jack decorating and actually papered a room at the farm, managing to ruin a good bit of paper by falling through it. However, they patched it up and the tear wasn't all that noticeable. He stayed at that job, playing havoc among the chippings until Jack was called up early in the war and the business closed down for the duration. It was about this time the Belvoir Estates gave him the job of looking after the ram. This was a pump over a spring housed in a small brick building in a field at the bottom of the allotments, called the 'Waineys', in School Lane. It pumped fresh water up to a tank in a farmyard not far from us and we were lucky, amongst others on our street, to have a tap in the back yard supplied from this source. Tom had to see that the pump was well-primed for working otherwise the tank would run dry and we would find an irate vicar on our front doorstep demanding to see Tommy. Why had his tank run dry? The simple answer was that Tommy had neglected his duty. Later, mains water was brought to the village and slowly water closets and bathrooms were put into the larger houses, but the cottages managed with primitive plumbing for many years.

# 19

## Early War Years

The Women's Land Army had been formed. Now girls, mostly from the towns, in their Aertex shirts, heavy green jerseys, wide khaki breeches, thick knee socks and heavy shoes, appeared working in the fields. Their uniforms were topped by a wide-brimmed, fawn felt hat. Miss Molly joined them and continued to run her own poultry farm and became quite a well-known person in this field. Apart from the housework I now had to give a hand with the farm work at busy times. I walked behind the horse hoe holding the wooden handles, while Alf, the waggoner, led the horse straight and true down the rows of young root crops. In the summer during the haymaking season I would ride on the horse rake, holding the reins myself and driving the horse up and down the hay field gathering up the hay with the rakes behind me lowered. I drew it along until I had a goodly pile in the tines, then pulled the lever and released it all in neat rows across the field ready for the people with hay forks to come along and pull it together into cocks. Later the wooden sweep would come along and pull it altogether in larger heaps called cobs. This was left to finish drying out whilst the reaper was busy in another field and the raking, cocking and cobbing would begin all over again. After all this, one fine day along would come the wagons and horses, and all the hay would be loaded up and taken to the stack yard and tossed into neat, fragrant stacks to keep for winter feed. Autumn, and potato picking time. I wasn't too keen on helping here, but it was essential to get all the food gathered in quickly and in good condition. So it was all hands to the fields. On top of all this were the household chores and poultry feeding and the knowledge that if one worked on a farm one would never be called up into the forces or any other war job. So leaving or doing anything else seemed out of the question.

We were all issued with identity cards and had to carry these around with us all the time. We heard of Anderson shelters being erected in

London and other places in case of air raids. The Women's Auxiliary Air Force and the Women's Royal Naval Service were set up. At home the Local Defence Volunteers were formed. Groups of men from every village around banded together and were issued with various weapons and uniforms and trained to defend their area should the Germans invade. Dad joined these and took his turn on duty at the especially vulnerable parts around Croxton. Their company HQ was at the Priory, Knipton, but Platoon 4, to which Dad belonged, had their operational HQ at Croxton Post Office. Their role being to 'Defend Croxton Kerrial and deny the main road, Grantham to Melton Mowbray, to the enemy.' Later they were called the Home Guard and much later still, affectionately, 'Dad's Army'. The Institute was allocated as the First Aid Post and the vicarage was the Decontamination Centre.

Not everyone had a telephone then. The available phones at that time being at the post office, vicarage and police house. Small, round concrete buildings called pillboxes were set up at strategic points by the side of all roads. One was built in the big field at the Lodge and a unit of soldiers was encamped down by the reservoir to man the guns should the enemy attempt to take the countryside by force. Nobody ever thought seriously about that happening around here and, of course, luckily it never did. The great searchlight at the base there fingered the sky at night, seeking with others any enemy aircraft, which happened to pass over to more important targets.

# 20

## Rationing Begins

The early 1940s saw great frosts and snows. Ponds were frozen over and roads blocked. Tom spent a lot of time learning to skate on Swallow Hole and the park ponds, becoming a real dab hand at it before the thaw finally set in. Snow at the farm was five or six feet deep. No tradesmen could get through; neither could the lorry get through to collect the milk, men couldn't get to work and I was at home suffering from flu and very bad chilblains. Dad, as a postman, was having a very difficult time. Mail vans were late getting through with the letters from Grantham, then he had to deliver all round the village and outlying farms on foot, a wearying time all round. When I felt well enough to go back to work I managed to get a lift in the mail van round by Knipton to the farm and what a hair-raising, bumpy ride it was! The field road was still cut off as far as cycling was concerned, nevertheless I had to plod home in the evening through the deep drifts that covered the roads.

About this time Tom left Jack Wildman to work as an assistant to the surveyor on the Ironstone, making himself useful in the office and carrying the theodolite when they went out surveying. Maisie was in hospital and the round of visiting was taking place once more. She had taken well to knitting and was busy making jumpers and cardigans. And also knitting toys, which sometimes she would manage to sell to friends.

Food rationing began and books of tokens were issued and everyone was required to register with a certain grocer and butcher. He deleted the food token each week and allowed customers a small portion of rationed food. It was never my lot to have to deal with rationing, my mother catered for us all at home, and Mrs Shipman at the farm. Farmers were usually well provided for from their land. Old hens were used for the pot and their eggs. They were allowed to keep one pig for the house and although all the milk had to be sent to the dairy they managed to keep a good basinful for themselves. When it had settled overnight the cream was skimmed off and used on porridge or cereal at breakfast. Wooden platforms were built at the farm gates and every morning the milk was taken down on a trolley in large, shining churns and left on them ready for the milk lorry to come along, then they were taken off to the local dairy.

Bees were kept at the Lodge in the orchard, so each year an amount of sugar was allowed to make up the syrup for their feeding, sugar also was allowed for jam making and preserving, which all contributed to self-sufficiency.

Rabbits were very plentiful too in the fields and made a tasty meal roasted with fresh herbs from the garden. Mrs Shipman used to make potted rabbit. After skinning and cleaning it would be boiled in a pot with a piece of fat bacon until the flesh fell from the bones. She would then put it through the mincer, flavouring it with salt, pepper and a little nutmeg, then into little dishes it would go, its top smoothed off and covered in melted butter. Served at the table with a sprig of fresh parsley on top and eaten with toast or homemade bread and butter, it was a meal fit for a queen. Lots of rabbits were caught in the harvest fields. When the binder was on its last strip of corn to be cut, men would be standing round with dogs and guns waiting for the little animals to make a dash for safety before they were caught in the cruel blades. Alas, if the blades didn't get them guns or dogs did and they made a welcome supplement to the meat ration.

In the autumn rabbiting days were organised affairs, farmers and friends gathering together and setting off with dogs and guns for a day's sport. Keeping the rabbit population down then was a necessity. There were hundreds of them and they could devastate a field of young corn or a vegetable garden. The men would come home muddy and wet in the foggy and often frosty darkening afternoon, dozens of rabbits strung on long poles by their back legs. By the light of stable lanterns they would set about gutting their catch in the crew yard, then back on their poles again the rabbits would all be put down in the cellar until market day when they would be taken to the nearest town and sold, no doubt at a good price. After they had gone I had to go down to the cellar and scrub up any puddles of blood, which had drained from the little creatures during their stay. A job I disliked intensely.

Another form of food, which was very much liked in those days, was custard made from the beastings, or beslings as some old folks called it. This was the first milk from the cow after the birth of a calf, baked like egg custard in the oven with sugar added. It made a nutritious meal. All this with the garden full of vegetables and the orchard full of fruit, a farm wasn't a bad place to be in wartime.

Clothing coupons were issued and had to be exchanged when clothes or household linen were needed. Utility furniture made its appearance – very functional and without frills or furbelows. Likewise utility buses were on the road with wooden slatted seats and no upholstery; all comforts sacrificed to the war effort.

New brides setting up home found things very difficult. They saved their coupons and begged and borrowed from friends to get enough for a new wedding outfit. White weddings were out, though one or two brides I knew hired their own traditional wedding dresses and their bridesmaids' dresses. Food rations were hoarded up so that there could be a 'bit of a do' on the great day. Many whose bridegrooms were in the forces continued to live at home with their parents and some were in the forces themselves. Young couples rushed to tie the knot before the bridegroom was sent overseas and many never met up again until the war was over, and a great many never saw each other again.

As soon as Tom was old enough to ride a motorbike on the roads he acquired an old Panther and was able to develop his interest in girls and dancing. One evening he said he would take me to dance at Eaton on the pillion. So all dressed up we set off through the rainy evening, me hanging on for dear life. All went well until we rounded the first corner in the village. There the wheels hit a large, sloppy cowpat and away the bike went in one direction whilst we went the other, landing heavily on the wet, muddy road. Tom picked himself up and rushed quickly to the motorbike where it lay on its side, its engine still running. "Not too badly damaged," he said. My stockings were torn and my skirt muddy, but except for a bloody knee I was not hurt. We thought we had come a cropper without anyone seeing us, but a voice from the gateway of a field called, "Ayer all right?" It turned out to be someone I knew slightly. He kindly took us to his house and we cleaned ourselves up. I discarded my torn stockings and we decided to continue to the dance. As usual we enjoyed ourselves and the evening quickly passed, time to go home. Tom appeared at my side, "I say G.," he said, "I've got to take Gordon home, you wait here till I come back." I was a bit apprehensive about being left, especially as the bike was a bit bent in places and I wondered if he would ever get back for me. However, eventually he arrived and once again I got astride the pillion and away we went. As aforesaid certain things were bent and the lights weren't working, but we had to get home. Up Branston Lings and down Croxton Lings we went. A policeman pushing his bike up the hill, no doubt our neighbour, shouted to us but we didn't stop. We careered onwards, up Dry Bank Hill and up and down the Switchback Hills, past the waterspout and the Peacock and we were home. We parked the motorbike in the top hovel and I put my torn stockings in the rag bag, and far as we were concerned that was that. We had no intention of telling our mother, but years later she mentioned it and laughingly said she had known all the time. We had reckoned without the village grapevine!

# 21

# Nursing and a Wedding

As a follow up to the First Aid and Home nursing lectures I had to do a number of hours as an auxiliary nurse in Melton Mowbray Hospital. Eventually I reported there for a few hours and was put on the private ward. It didn't seem much different from domestic work, switching on radios and arranging flowers etc. and I didn't see much point in continuing with it. However, later on I received a letter asking me to go and finish my training, so I decided to do it all in one lump sum and live in at the hospital.

This time I was put on the women's ward, which was much better. I learned how to give out bedpans and give bed baths, take pulses and temperatures, which I always found difficult. The strictness in the nursing profession then I found very inhibiting and didn't really enjoy hospital life, although I did like being with and looking after the patients. One old lady wrote me a special poem, and there was an old gentleman I still remember. He was very ill in a side ward and one day I was sent to sit by him for a while. He was determined to get dressed and go home, "You get my clothes, nurse," he wheedled, "If you don't, I will," and he started to push the bedclothes back. I got worried, I knew he couldn't get very far but if he got agitated and fell out of bed I would be in dire trouble. "Where are your clothes?" I said. "In my locker drawer," was the reply. "Oh Mr A., I can't possibly get them for you, Sister would be so cross with me and you wouldn't want to get me into trouble would you?" "No, no nurse," he said, "I wouldn't want to do that," and he settled wearily back on his pillows. I relaxed with a sigh of relief and felt that I had managed that situation quite well. "You're a toff," he said, "A real toff." The next time I came on duty he had passed away, and his widow stood in lonely grief outside his closed ward door.

Some of the auxiliary nurses used to think that the paid nurses resented them, thinking that they were only playing at nursing to avoid being called up into the forces or other war work. One Sister in particular made it very tough for me and I feel if she had been kinder I might have taken more kindly to nursing as a career. Towards the end of this spell of training my friend Jean rang me to say that her fiancé Ted was coming home on leave at the weekend and they planned to get married on the Saturday, could I be bridesmaid? How I was going to manage it at such short notice I didn't really know, but manage it I must. It meant bearding the Sister in her den to make a request. Two nurses said they would go with me for moral support. We met Sister in the corridor and I timidly asked if I could speak to her, "Please could I work right through the remaining hours I had to do without any time off and leave earlier than I should have done?" She didn't take kindly to the idea and the wrath of the gods descended on me. "Whatever were you doing before you came here, Nurse Woods?" she shouted. "I worked on a farm, Sister," I said. "Well then you'd better go back to your farm, hadn't you?" she said scathingly. I felt about as big as a ha'penny, as with a swish of her starched skirts she continued her journey along the corridor. Anyway I finished my required hours of training and packed my bags and boarded a bus for home, shaking the dust of that particular hospital off my feet forever.

Home again I found that all arrangements had been made for Jean's wedding at Croxton Church. Luckily I had only just bought a new grey coat and blue, schoolgirl type, felt hat. Jean said they would do nicely. She had a navy suit and a Robin Hood type felt hat and we both wore medium-heeled, square-toed shoes that were the fashion at that time.

On Saturday afternoon of December 13th I got all dressed up and went along to Jean's house in the Nook. Up in her bedroom we put the finishing touches to our outfits with a pink carnation corsage. Being ready in good time we perched ourselves by the little window looking across the gardens to the main road, up which Ted's car would travel before turning into Middle Street for the church. We just caught a glimpse of it as it sped by. Great excitement! My turn to be driven up to church, and then Jean and her father to follow. The afternoon was dull, but not for us. Jean and her father arrived and I followed them up the aisle, and there was Ted, young and shy in his able seamen's uniform with a white satin ribbon and a white carnation at the neck of his sailor's jersey. The ceremony over we all made our way back to the Nook where her parents entertained the guests, whilst Jean, Ted and myself went to Grantham to have photographs taken at Walter Lee's studio on the High Street. After this there was a quick celebratory drink in a hotel with some of Jean's office colleagues. Darkness was falling as the taxi took us back to Croxton and the waiting guests. The bride and groom weren't going away until the next day so after everyone had left the reception they insisted on seeing me home. Later they told me they had waited about in the Nook afterwards until all of the family had gone to bed and they could creep up to their room unobserved.

One day later on I met the vicar's wife, who meaning to be kind and cheery said, "Well, that's Jean married, never mind, it will be your turn next." "Not yet if I can help it," I thought, "I want, I want...," but what did I want? I had a feeling that whatever it was I wasn't going to find it in Croxton.

The honeymoon over, Ted went back to his minesweeper and Jean continued to live at home, so we were able to continue our good friendship.

## 22

# Croxton Social Life Peps Up a Bit

Croxton Park was taken over by some big business man who came to live in the house. The stables and outbuildings being turned into offices and his staff evacuated from London to occupy them. Something to do with armaments they said, all very hush, hush. One of his clerks was lodged at the farmhouse in the lane from where we fetched our milk. Soon I met Stanley and we became friends, though I didn't want to get seriously involved or take him home. However, we went for a walk one Sunday evening and got caught in a downpour. We sheltered as long as we could under a tree, but the rain never stopped, and there was nothing for it but to take him home with me. We were both like drowned rats. I opened the front door and called in, much to Mum's amusement, "It's no good Mum, I'll have to bring him in, we're both soaked." So, Stanley became a regular visitor to our house, with his smart suits and his cockney accent. He liked nothing better than to sit by our fire and make piles of toast. He and Maisie got on like a house on fire. His mother came to stay for a weekend at the farm and I went up to meet her. "You must have a magnet inside you," she said, "You pull him away down that lane every spare minute." I'd got a feeling she wasn't too pleased about me. We went to dances now in aid of the war effort. Stan learnt to play 'In the Mood' on the piano with great gusto. Film shows were put on in the school showing how 'Careless talk costs lives' and 'Walls have ears'. One or two village men disappeared into the forces, but village life remained peaceful. After a while Stan decided to join up and offered himself for service with the RAF. He was soon called away and ended up in the RAF. His regiment landed in the Middle East, from where I was kept well supplied with letters, photographs and a proposal of marriage. Somehow I was tempted, but in the end said that I'd like to wait until he came home so I could see him again. Not having been all that smitten before he went away I didn't see how I could suddenly want to marry him. They do say absence makes the heart grow fonder.

An airfield was built at Saltby, housing a bomber squadron and some of the RAF personnel visited Croxton pub and the dances which were held in the Institute, and they certainly livened up village life. Hetty and I met two very nice young men and went to quite a few dances with them. Hetty's brother-in-law used to take us in his car, bring us all home and we would finish off with supper in either of our houses. Dick and I spent quite a bit of time together, but no one thought overmuch about the future. He was an air gunner in the plane and his job was a dangerous one, to make the understatement of the year. We were great partners on the dance floor and, as it was Christmas time when he was around, really enjoyed the dances that were organised. However, one at Waltham turned out to be a disappointment though. We arrived as usual in our taxi, had one or two dances then Dick disappeared. "Oh well," I thought, "He's just gone for a drink," but all through the evening he didn't turn up and I got really worried. Nearly time for the last waltz and there he was, what a mess he looked. Vacant-eyed, his uniform and face covered in mud and gravel. What on earth had happened to him? Bill, Hetty's brother-in-law, was looking after him and ushered us all into his car and drove us home. It was a silent ride. Bill drove under the open shed where he parked his car and we all sat clamped to our seats as the sound of cascading water poured from somewhere. Deathly hush. We all froze, it couldn't be, not Dick. We all knew he was drunk and fairly incapable but... Great waves of laughter broke as we realised it was a cow next door relieving itself and we breathed freely again! We got Dick into the house and all had something to eat, the men keeping an eye on him. I went home to my bed feeling a bit let down, but realising even then that these lads were under great strain and some of them not really enjoying their wartime roles. No wonder that sometimes they let off steam by their excesses. The next evening Dick was at our door apologising profusely and asking me to go to the cinema that evening to make up for his lapse at the dance. Apparently he had felt unwell and had gone outside for fresh air, he said. He had sat on a fence and every time he had tried to get off, the ground came up and hit him.

Later on their familiar faces disappeared from the social scene and we never really knew what happened to them. Had they been posted or worse still had they been blasted out of the night skies by the enemy, we had no way of finding out.

# 23

# Extended Families

At the beginning of the war thousands of school children, mothers with babies and toddlers, and sick and handicapped people had all been evacuated from London and the big cities to the safety of rural areas. School children in the charge of teachers and other adult helpers, boarding trains with labels in their lapels, gas masks round their necks, and little bundles of belongings in their hands. All being carried away to strange places and strange people in, what a leading newspaper of the day called, an unprecedented exodus. The host families at the end of their journey welcoming them into their homes and trying to make them as comfortable as possible, but a lot didn't settle down to their strange new life and gradually drifted back home.

The 'quiet war' lasted to early summer of 1940 then trouble began in earnest. The German air force launched its attack on Britain, mainly aiming for London and what was to become known as the Battle of Britain raged in the skies over the South coast. Spitfires and Hurricanes battled night and day to beat off the marauding enemy planes. Occasionally the Luftwaffe managed to get as far as Grantham and several bombs were dropped, most hitting private houses, and missing altogether their prime targets the ammunition factories. One bomb dropped in Denton, which caused a large crater but no damage was done to any property, nor anyone hurt. Maisie was in the hospital once when the bombs dropped in the town, but they were a distance away and no harm was done. One summer day I remember standing out in the lane at the farm watching a dogfight in the sky, high up white vapour trails crossed and criss-crossed the blue, as two tiny specks, 'one of ours' and 'one of theirs' fought it out, until one peeled away closely followed by the other and out of sight.

Eventually this stage of the war was won, thanks to the brave fighter pilots and their too few nifty little planes. The enemy was driven back for a while, but more horror was to come, Hitler launched his great bombers in their hundreds over our towns and cities and, once again, in October more evacuees were sent out of London. This time a few arrived in Croxton, a mother and her three little boys being billeted on the farm. They arrived on a Saturday afternoon in October, my day off and I was in Grantham, but I went to work on Sunday and there they all were. Three lovely little boys, Terry the eldest four years old, Frankie chubby and curly haired, and the baby only eight weeks old. He had been born under the table during a bombing raid, what a traumatic experience for his mother.

She was tall and gaunt and wary eyed, trying to come to terms with her new surroundings. The old schoolroom was given over to them and two bedrooms, and for a while there was a strangeness on both sides during the settling in period. For much of the time Mrs Edwards was quiet and withdrawn, but the children settled in well, and great credit must go to the Shipman family who took these strangers into their home and coped with such disruption in their lives. This goes too for all the other people who gave sanctuary to those in need of shelter and comfort during that dreadful time. Later, when she was feeling more settled Mrs. Edwards would sing to the children in the kitchen, the old walls would resound with 'Knees up Moover Braene, Knees up Moover Braene' and other cockney choruses, and loud laughter. "You don't 'arf talk funny," she said to me one day: I expect our Leicester voices did seem as strange to her ears as her cockney did to ours.

The children grew and blossomed with the country air and country food, and became quite the little poultry feeders. The baby was christened at Croxton Church, and given the names John James, and what a lovely little baby he was. Sometimes I would take them out for walks in the afternoons but mostly their mother trailed off with them, either to the post office up at Branston or the shop at Knipton, I think she found things very quiet in the country, but she too was looking better for her new way of life.

Once or twice their father visited them for a day or two, but had to get back to his job in London and during all the time at the farm they didn't see much of him. They had a daughter Lily who had been evacuated to somewhere in Devon, but we didn't meet her till after the war. Life was busier than ever at the farm, food production became of major importance and 'Dig for Victory' became the slogan of the day. People replaced their flowerbeds with cabbage patches and every available piece of garden produced some form of food. Iron railings were removed from house fronts and from around monuments, and housewives sent their metal utensils to make into armaments. Belts were tightened to meet the challenge of the great forces ranged against us.

More young men were called up from the village and the girls too started to join the forces as they reached the age groups for call-up to war work. Most girls in the village worked in the munition factories at Grantham, working in shifts round the clock to produce the much needed guns and tanks. London and the larger cities were being bombed nightly, the news reels at the cinema showing us just how terrible the devastation and loss of life were.

One dark night we looked from our front doorstep towards the Park and saw in the far distant sky a terrible glow and flashes of gunfire, we watched the distant enemy action with awed wonder. "Who was catching it now?" we thought, "Must be Coventry." High overhead, bombers droned, were they ours or theirs? Search lights frantically swept the sky but here, close at home, all was quiet, only over there the drama was being enacted as we sombrely made our way into our safe home and bed. In the morning we found out for sure that Coventry had suffered grievous destruction and loss of life, even the cathedral being reduced to a heap of rubble.

After about ten months at the farm Mrs Edwards got restless and wanted to go back to London and, quite naturally, to her husband. Arrangements were made for her to leave and she wanted to take Frankie back with her, leaving Terry and John at the farm, and away they went. Before long she wrote to say Frankie couldn't settle and was having a terrible time could Mrs. Shipman have him back again? Of course, he could come back, but after some thought Mrs. Shipman decided that without their mother she couldn't cope with all three children so it was arranged that Terry would live at the farm cottage with the cowman and his wife, and Frankie would come to live with us in Croxton, Johnny staying at the farm. So the boys all found good homes, and became country children – indeed Frankie was welcomed with open arms by Mum, and Maisie undertook to make him her special charge. I think Dad was always sceptical as to whether this arrangement was the best thing for the family, but he had no say against the feminine forces ranged against him.

About this time my forms came through from the government to Mrs. Shipman, which she had to fill in to vouch for my job being a reserved occupation. Feeling in her heart that I should be doing other things, she felt she should give me a chance to have the choice of staying at the farm or going for other kinds of war work. She gave me the form to fill in myself, at last the chance for release from the job I had done for nearly nine years. What should I do? Things were quite well at home, Dad was as well as he ever would be, Tom was still

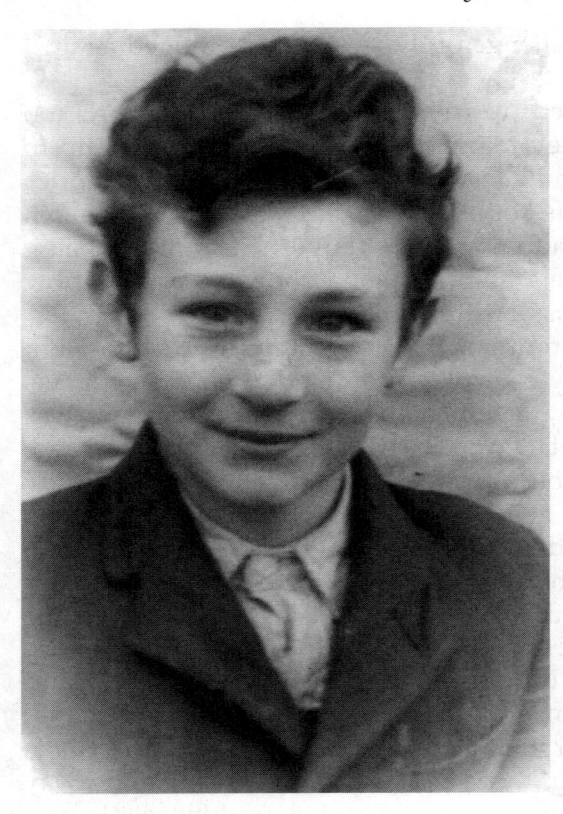

*Frank Edwards – evacuated.*

at home and Mum taken up with Maisie and Frankie. I felt that if I was ever to make the break it was now, so I boldly filled in my form with household duties being my occupation, and these certainly didn't come under the reserved occupation umbrella. Mother was upset that I wanted to get away, but I think Dad was pleased that at last I would have the chance to do what I wanted with my life, and I felt that he approved. Filling in the forms, I put as my first choice for war work the Women's Auxiliary Air Force, still thinking in the back of my mind about my blonde airman. Maybe, if I was accepted for the Waaf, by some quirk of fate I would somehow meet him again. My second choice being the Auxiliary Territorial Service, the deed was done and the form duly posted to the powers that be. In no time at all it seemed that I got notice to attend at St John's Hall in Grantham for my medical examination with a view to joining the ATS. I felt very disappointed at first that it wasn't the Waaf but by doing my usual 'adapting to circumstances act', I felt that the ATS was better than a factory.

I duly presented myself with lots of other girls at St John's Hall on the appointed day and with the rest sat through my intelligence test, then passed before several doctors. The last one going deeply into why were my ankles so knobbly and why were my legs bruised? I explained about my illness as a baby, and said I expect I had been clumsy and knocked myself. This didn't altogether convince her that I was now healthy, so she sent me back round all the doctors once again, they pronounced me A1 and I was through the hurdle, now I had to await my calling up papers. Little pricks of conscience and sadness stirred in me sometimes that I soon would be leaving, but I was sure I was doing right and all would be well. It didn't take long for my papers to come through and I left Croxton Lodge with a tinge of sadness. Mrs Shipman gave me a pigskin writing case, Miss Molly a fountain pen and Master Billy a manly purse. I went round all my friends saying goodbye, lastly calling in at the church which had been the centre of my life for so many years. On June 26th 1942 I left Croxton for Glen Parva Barracks near Leicester and became a member of the Auxiliary Territorial Service.

# Part III

## The ATS

# 24

# Outward Bound

The bus moved away from the bus stop and gathered speed as it set off down the road and around the corner by the Peacock, past the horse pond, wash dyke, and cascading waterspout. Up and down the hills and along the straight, carrying me away from Croxton to a new and unknown world beyond. In the sunlit June afternoon the old familiar fields and tracks spread out below me, I bid a silent farewell to the old life and looked forward to the new with excitement and not a little apprehension.

The usual railway ticket had been sent to enable me to travel free to Glen Parva barracks but having the bus pass down the main road at the end of our street made things much easier and I felt I could cope with a bus journey rather than the unfamiliar train ride, and would be there in half the time. The words of the old hymn came to me as I was borne along 'Forth in Thy Name, O Lord, I go', for I had no doubt at all that the Lord travelled with me, and I found that to be my strength come what may.

Leicester was a foreign country to me, I had only been there once before on a Sunday school pantomime outing, now we were pulling into its busy bus terminal. Where did I go from here, which way did I go now? After making enquiries I found that I needed to be outside the Midland Station to get a bus out to Glen Parva. Clanking trams, traffic and people surged round me. I took a good grip on my handbag and case and made my way as directed, and soon found myself outside the station entrance where in the middle of the road stood cattle-like pens where people queued for buses going out to various destinations. Not many people waiting there, I found my bus stop and there to my surprise was a friend's mother waiting for another bus. I was so pleased to see someone I knew, the world had suddenly become a big and lonely place. We chatted away until looking across into the dim interior of the station forecourt I could see an army truck pulled in and a group of girls like myself, in civilian clothes and with small cases, standing round an ATS Corporal who was ticking off names from a list in her hand. "That's where you want to be, I think," said my companion, I thought so too and dashed across the road to join the group. The Corporal took me under her wing as I enquired as to their destination; she ran her finger down her list, "Woods, G.," she said and ticked my name. "Right," she ordered, "Everyone into the truck." We obeyed and clambered into the back of the high vehicle and took our seats on either side under the canvas roof reminiscent of the old carrier's cart. We sat clutching our cases on our knees, a silent bunch, as we bumped and swayed along the road out of the city and finally in through the barrack gates. The truck stopped, "Everybody out," yelled the Corporal and we leaped awkwardly down onto the tarmac outside the Guardroom. We looked curiously about us; clusters of tall, brick Victorian buildings surrounded us, to the left barrack rooms once housing the Leicestershire Regiment now taken over by the ATS as a training establishment. To the right were the offices and storerooms and further on still the creeper-covered Officers' Mess. In front of us was the Square, a sacred piece of ground not to be trodden on lightly or wantonly. Beyond that a great expanse of lawn, trees and rose beds, all very spruce and orderly.

"Get into threes," our Corporal ordered and we all shuffled into place, "Quick march," and away we went along the broad asphalt path between the green and the rose beds, and on into the unseen area at the back of the barracks where there were lots of hutments called 'spiders'. Our party was allocated a hut and our beds. These were placed down each side of the room in a head-to-toe formation and, of course, I got one with the head to the middle of the room. They looked funny little beds and seemed half size, but we found they closed up concertina-wise to the wall when not in use to leave more space in the room. The mattress was made up of three different sections called biscuits, these with the blankets and pillows were neatly piled at the end of the bed and we were issued with a pair of white sheets and a pillowcase. Later we were shown how to make them up and, in the morning, how to barrack them, as it was called.

The whole place smelt of new wood and polish, all shiny, spick and span. We were told to leave our things by our beds and form up again outside, we were being sent for our FFI to the MI. This was the Medical Inspection room and we were to be examined to make sure we were 'Fit and Free from Infection'. We piled into the waiting room with its large expanse of shining floor and wooden forms around the walls. "Everything off except your pants," was the next order. "Goodness," I thought, looking round. One or two girls started pulling their dresses over their heads, "Oh well, something we have to get used to," I supposed and began to strip off to my peach satin French knickers. What a sight for sore eyes, a crowd of girls, all sorts and all sizes, large and small, pendulant and flat, some trying to cover their modesty as best they could, others nonchalantly flaunting. We all stood in a line to pass before the doctor, she turned us round and expertly flicked our panties and we were passed on to the MI Corporal who ruffled through our hair, would these indignations never cease? Dressed again we were ushered through a connecting door to the dental surgeries where our teeth were inspected and our dental hygiene assessed.

Outside again in the sunshine and we were on our way to the stores to be kitted out with our uniform: tunic, skirt, shirts, cap, vests, large khaki bloomers, pink corsets, bras, khaki stockings, two pairs of shoes, plimsolls to go with our PE kit, a greatcoat and kitbag, not to mention brass-cleaning and shoe-cleaning materials, steel helmet and respirator. All this was dumped in front of us on the long counter down the centre of the room by an ATS store girl, more or less getting our sizes right. Luckily, I was stock size so didn't have much trouble getting fitted up. We humped all these things in our arms as best we could and made our way back to our spiders. Once there an orgy of trying on and adjustment took place, we inspected each other, what a lot of raw rookies we looked! We were each given a card, ready printed, to sign and send off to our parents to say that we had arrived safely, which was posted right away. Our Corporal showed us how to polish our brass buttons, our badges, and our shoes so that in time we would see our faces in them. That day seemed a very long way away to us, would we ever feel at ease in our new life?

At last it was teatime, all outside once more and we marched to the cookhouse. We had all been issued with a knife, a fork, a spoon and a pint pot and kept these with us at all times. We filed into the large, noisy building and along the serving counters where mess orderlies dished out the piping-hot food. Carrying it to the scrubbed trestle tables we ate our first communal meal. By now our individual reserve was breaking down and tentative moves towards friendship were being made. Having finished our meal we swished our eating utensils and mugs through great pans of hot water by the door and made once again for our huts. It all seemed to be coming and going, but after tea we were free to go off and find the Naafi. Here we could spend our cigarette and sweet coupons, have a cup of tea and a chat and try to come to terms with the strange life in which we found ourselves. Some of us had joined voluntarily and looked forward to it as an experience, but others who had been conscripted seemed disgruntled and felt it was robbing them of a slice of their youth. That night we laid ourselves down to sleep on our hard beds in unfamiliar surroundings and not without a few homesick thoughts in our minds and silent tears into the pillow.

# 25

# Rookie Days

In no time at all the Corporal's voice sounded in our ears, "Out of bed, everybody," and so began our first full day in our new life. After our ablutions we were marched down to the cookhouse for breakfast and our three weeks' basic training had begun. Days of lectures on hygiene, ATS administration and gas detection etc. The gas detection bit I already knew a little about, having learned it in my time in the Civil Defence. We were required to don our respirators and enter a gas chamber for a few seconds, slightly open the face piece and sniff mustard gas to acquaint us with the smell should we ever be involved with that deadly weapon. On the Square we quickly had to learn our right hand from our left, or rather our feet! Some of us wondered if we ever would as the Sergeant's voice rang out 'F, I, F, I' which we quickly had to interpret as 'left, right, left, right'!

Gradually we were licked into shape, and in no time at all were marching and wheeling, standing easy and at ease, sticking our chests out and our bottoms in to the rapped-out order of the training NCOs: 'Bags of swank, bags of swank'.

Vaccinations and inoculations put fear into our hearts as we paraded before the Medical Officer with our sleeves rolled up and waited for the sharp prick in our upper arms. One particular morning we were told to leave our beds down as we were to have another jab which would make us feel rather ill and need to get our heads down, terrifying. Once again we filed before the doctor and we were soon back in the hut and relaxing on our beds, by evening we were feeling very ill indeed, moaning and groaning filled the hut and temperatures rose and delirium set in. I felt like death and I wasn't one of the worst, all I could think of in the sweaty heat was my mother's voice saying 'Goodnight and God bless you, I hope you'll have a good night's rest and waken up well in the morning.' Eventually things quietened down and sleep took over and in due course I did wake up feeling alright, well nearly. We all had stiff arms and some had reacted badly to the serum and had to be taken to camp hospital. The after-effects did not last long and we were all up and about though not allowed to go out of camp for our first weekend.

Pay was a long, drawn-out affair, we were all marched down to Company Office to await our name being called, my initial being 'W' I had a longer wait than most. Then, smartly coming to attention, I marched briskly before the Commanding Officer, reported my name and number, took my pay in one hand and saluted with the other, a quick about-turn and away I went with the princely sum of eight shillings clutched in my hand. Badges, buttons and shoes had to shine for the occasion and uniforms pressed, but pride and confidence grew as we progressed through our rookie days.

After the first week we were allowed out of barracks for our free time, visiting the cinema in Wigston and sometimes in Leicester, but none of us from our hut strayed very far afield.

The day came when we all had to visit the Personnel Officer to determine what job we were best suited for. I was very pleased to find her easy to talk to and we got on well from the start. I had to say I hadn't had any particular training for anything, only housework, and had done my required voluntary hours in hospital for the Red Cross, having passed my First Aid and Home Nursing exams with top marks. I told her I didn't want to be a house orderly, she nodded understandingly and I left her feeling my future was in good hands.

Towards the end of our training we were all ordered on church parade and it was with a great feeling of pride as, led by the band of the Leicestershire Regiment, we swung out of the barrack gates and on to the Church of St Thomas at the bottom of the road. It didn't suit some of the girls, non-churchgoers who felt they had been forced to go, but I really enjoyed the experience.

The last week of our training saw me on the only route march on which I ever went and which I can't remember much about. Finally, our last kit inspection, we laid everything out on our beds as we had been trained to do, all neat and orderly, and stood to attention as our CO made her rounds with the Corporal of our hut. As they passed round they scanned our kit with an eagle eye and perhaps a brusque remark and moved quickly on, we could relax, all was well.

Now the big moment had arrived, the passing out parade. Much polishing and burnishing and clothes pressing, we were almost fully fledged ATS. Each squad under its own corporal paraded outside their hut and were duly marched off to the Square. Here we were all marched and countermarched before the brass hats, stood stiffly to attention as they slowly inspected our ranks, the tarmac surface of the Square shimmering in the heat of the July day. At last we were marched off and the big day was over, a rush to read Company Orders, had the postings come through? Yes, there they were pinned up on the notice board; I was to go to Derby, still not too far from home. First we were given spot leave and we happily left to rejoin our families. The days sped swiftly by, things for the moment were well at home. All too soon it was time to catch the bus again back to the barracks, meeting up with my companions of the last three weeks. The time had come for us all to pack our kitbags for the first time and to polish round our beds for the last time, we had come to the parting of the ways. We who were posted to Derby caught the train together and were on our way.

# 26

# Derby Days

An army truck was waiting for us at Derby Station, already loaded with girls being delivered to postings in and around Derby. Where would I be going? My enquiries were answered with, "Oh, you're going to Tresco." "What's Tresco?" I asked, nobody seemed inclined to enlighten me as to my eventual destination. The truck moved about from one place to another and at last into the suburbs, large houses in tree-lined roads and here turned into a gravel drive, 'Tresco' it said on a sign on the gatepost. So this was it, "Not bad, not bad at all," I thought, "What next?" It turned out to be a large requisitioned house standing in its own garden, this was to be my billet for some time. There was a corporal in charge who did the cooking and two house orderlies to help her and, at the most, about a dozen ATS all going about their particular duties at various army depots everyday. As it turned out I was to become a dental clerk/orderly at another requisitioned house in another part of town. There were two other girls already in the billet attached to the Dental Corporal, who didn't seem all that pleased at having a new girl to cope with, but I wasn't unduly worried, I knew eventually we would all work together quite well. We had to catch a bus to work each morning, as we neared the road on which the Dental Centre stood, both girls stood up ready to get off, "You have to jump for it," they told me, "or you will be carried up the road." "Oh Lord!" I thought, I hadn't travelled on city buses much anyway, let alone jumped off a moving one but I knew I had to do it or perish in the attempt. The bus slowed slightly as it rounded the bend, Cathie and Julie were poised on the step, ready to jump, and away they went, I followed immediately and landed on my feet, rather shaken, but the right way up. Each morning I got more adept at this athletic procedure and soon could land as unconcernedly as the rest of them.

The first dental officer I worked with was a Capt. Smith, he occupied a small surgery at the back of the house and to my surprise still used the old foot-pedal drill for filling teeth. It was he who taught me how to mix linings and amalgams, sterilize instruments and make up patients' record cards. Every now and again when his foot got tired I used to treadle the machine, occasionally losing rhythm, which would cause a few painful jerks in the poor old patients' mouths. It was a relief all round when an electrically driven drill was installed. Eventually we were all moved round and I was allocated to another officer in a large surgery at the front of the house.

Our patients were young soldier recruits from local training camps. They were brought to the Dental Centre in trucks and marched into the waiting room where they sat with loud mouthed bravado or petrified into silence by the thought of sitting in the dental chair. In turn we had to call each one by name up to the surgeries from the top of the main staircase. However, like all aspects of this new life I soon got used to it and enjoyed my job, as Dad used to say, I really fell on my feet. The dental officers were all gentlemen and looked after us like Dutch uncles. Most of them had their wives in rented accommodation in town and went home to them after work each day. Being dentists at heart they didn't exact any army discipline from us and the atmosphere between everyone was relaxed and friendly. Although we were attached to Markeaton camp we went home to our requisitioned house so were not bothered much about attending army activities. However, this changed for a while when we moved to another house nearer the camp, then the CO decreed that the 'dental girls' went into camp every morning before going to work and do a stint with the rest of the soldiers and ATS on the Square. With much grumbling we appealed to our dental officers to get us off this chore, nothing doing, except to say that they needed us in the surgeries by 8.30 every morning. We would go down into camp and to the Square beside the lake and here we would fall in with the rest of HQ Company and under the orders of a male sergeant major would drill, march and countermarch whilst the swans on the lake eyed our antics with regal interest. It was a beautiful place, some mornings a mist would shroud the water and the camp buildings, and the everyday sounds of army life seemed to be muffled in cotton wool. As we needed to be away early before the drill was finished there would come a point in time when we were halted and drawn up in our ranks, the SM would bawl out, "Dental girls, fall out," and three little khaki-clad figures would spring to attention, smartly salute, right turn and march off the Square. Quite an unnerving procedure in front of the whole of HQ Company standing at ease, and the overwhelming urge to run to the safety of the grass and trees at the edge of the Square needed all the discipline to which we had been trained, but it was worth it to get away to freedom. Our critics would say that the dental girls could get away with anything.

Things at home were carrying on much the same as usual. Maisie continued to knit toys and jumpers, sometimes selling them to friends. She, poor lass, spent her sixteenth birthday in hospital. Mum had received her calling-up papers with the rest of her age group, unbelievable really, but people were desperately needed for war work. She was never actually called to work anywhere other that at home, looking after Dad and Maisie in their constant ill health and Frankie, our evacuee. He had settled down well in Croxton and started school, becoming one of our family, all of us being very fond of him. Mother kept up a stream of letters to me, and I had quite a fan mail from all my friends, including letters from Stanley in the Middle East. Occasionally Mum would send me a parcel with an apple or orange and a packet of biscuits, very scarce commodities then, sometimes a neighbour would chip in and send a home-made cake. Kirby grips for our hair were in short supply, but Mum managed to scrounge some from somewhere. Some of the time I sent my shirts and collars home, she was a dab hand at washing and starching them, very smart indeed. Mrs Shipman would also send me parcels from Croxton Lodge of home-grown apples etc. and a book of stamps, very acceptable when writing so many letters.

In the camp there were dances in the Gym and ENSA concerts with well-known performers to cheer up the troops. Pat Kirkwood with her hit song 'O Johnny, O Johnny, How You Can Love' and an up-and-coming comedian Fred Neal are two that I remember very well. Sometimes, on Sunday, I would go out and find a church, but I can't say I ever found the congregation or parsons very friendly. Mostly our evenings were spent round the fire in the sitting room of our billet, writing letters home or listening to records on the gramophone. Vera Lynn singing 'There'll be Blue Birds over the White Cliffs of Dover' and other sentimental war songs.

The atmosphere in our house was very friendly, we were warm and well looked after and fairly free to come and go as we pleased. We three dental girls got on well together so it was particularly startling when we were all together one evening with Julie airing her views and having a good grumble, and Cathie suddenly screeched at her that she was "Blethering on like a pregnant woman," and snatching up the ink bottle threw it straight at Julie's head. There was a shocked silence as Julie ducked and the bottle smashed against the marble mantelpiece, the ink sliding down in little streams into the hearth. Julie ran sobbing from the room and Cathie moodily continued to write letters; bedtime came as a happy release to us all.

The kitchen was closed at 10 p.m. so any last drinks had to be made before then, unless we were out on a late pass we were always in bed in good time. Cathie, Julie and I shared a room, green boxes stood at the ends of our beds to house our kit instead of the tall, green lockers we had in camp. Furnishings were spartan but adequate. One night a week we had to clean and polish our room, and every so often the CO would appear and do a surprise inspection just to keep us on our toes. On the night of the ink bottle incident when Cathie and I went to bed Julie appeared to be asleep and nothing more was ever said about it, though weeks later we had every cause to remember and regret Cathie's hasty action.

Letters from home told me that Maisie and her friend Elsie had started work at the Red House at Knipton, once the hunting box of the Abel-Smiths, now an evacuated children's home. They cycled down there each day, so doing their bit towards the war effort.

By now Tom had decided he would like to join the Navy, so volunteered before his eighteenth birthday, thinking this would ensure that he would get into the force he really preferred. Alas, like me, he didn't get his first choice and was drafted into the Army. They were needing electricians badly and the REME had just been formed. Having had some electrical training he found himself eventually in their ranks as a regular soldier with twelve years' service ahead of him. He reported to Oadby Training Centre, near Leicester, a week before Christmas 1942, so for the first time in both our lives we were both away from home for the festive season. The highlight of the festivities in camp was Christmas Dinner with all the trimmings when soldiers and ATS ate together and the officers waited on us, but as Tom said in a letter home 'We really enjoyed ourselves but underneath it all we were wishing we were at home!' We received monetary gifts from Croxton Women's Institute and Tom got his first army pay of £1, and told Mum he would send home that which he didn't spend and she could save it for him! According to his letters he and some of his mates sang in Oadby Church Choir and joined the Carol Singers on their rounds. Sadly Maisie developed jaundice and had to go into hospital so Mum and Dad did not have a very happy time this year at all. Soon after Christmas both Tom and I managed to get a sleeping-out pass and were able to visit Maisie in hospital.

# 27

## Goodbye Derby

New Year 1943 and still a war on, the weather snowy and I set a trend by having my hair permed. We had to wear it an inch above our collars and most of us tied a band round our heads and rolled our hair round it, a very quick and efficient way of doing it. The hairdresser swept mine up round my head bringing it down into what she called a victory roll. It was met with approval from my friends who one after another decided to have theirs done too.

One evening Cathie and I came out of the cinema and decided to call in at a milk bar for light refreshment. The place was crowded and hot with standing room only, we unbuttoned our greatcoats and waited, more or less patiently, before pushing our way to the counter for a milk shake. Cathie, a great smoker, lit a cigarette and offered me one, I didn't really enjoy smoking but for once I took one. We finished our drinks and couldn't get out of the milk bar on to the street fast enough. We had only gone a few steps when two ATS redcaps stepped in front of us, I heard Cathie mutter something but didn't know what it was. "Fasten your greatcoats," was the police girl's first order, "and put out that cigarette," she snapped. Then I knew what Cathie had tried to tell me, she had quickly dropped her cigarette but I was still holding mine and was caught. They took my name etc. and a few days later I received a summons to Company Office on the charge of smoking in the street. It caused great amusement at the Dental Centre, Grace on a charge, and I was given dire warnings of what might happen to me in the way of punishments.

The day for my appearance before my Company Commander arrived and I had to get across Derby by bus to Markeaton camp. I had dreaded the thought of being given a spell in the cookhouse peeling spuds, but I wasn't unduly worried, the worst they could do was shoot me, I thought. The Orderly Sergeant was waiting for me outside Company Office. "Right, Woods," she said, "Take your titfer off." I removed my cap, a private was called as my guard, she marched in first, then me and the Sergeant behind me, we were halted and drawn up in a line in front of the CO. Vaguely I thought I had seen her as a patient but I couldn't be sure. The Sergeant read out the charge, "Being caught in the street holding a cigarette with greatcoat open." "Have you anything to say, Woods?" asked the officer. I looked straight at her and our eyes met and the battle was won. "Yes, Ma'am," I said smartly, "We were picked up rather quickly outside the milk bar and hadn't had time to button our coats, and what's more Ma'am, I'm not really a smoker, I forgot I was holding a cigarette." "Well, Woods," she answered, "You do seem to have been picked up rather quickly. No charge this time, but remember, Woods, it's the little things in life that count." "Yes, Ma'am," I said and I felt like adding, "I've heard that all my life." I was marched out again and was a free woman and welcomed back to the Dental Centre with open arms. It had been quite an experience, and Cathie, having dropped her cigarette in the nick of time, got off, as you might say, scot-free!

Round about this time I arrived at the billet after work one day to be met in the hall by a distraught Cathie. "Grace, come in here," she said in her urgent Scotch brogue, opening the sitting room door she pulled me in. "Oh Grace, Julie's had a baby," she said dramatically. We stared at each other, we just couldn't believe it. Julie had been working alongside us all this time, dragging backwards and forwards to the Dental Centre, and none of us had suspected a thing. Our minds went back to the evening in the sitting room when Cathie had said she was 'blethering on like a pregnant woman'. "I wish I'd never said that," she moaned, "I had no idea!" It appeared she had been taken off to hospital very ill indeed and her parents had been sent for, no other details were passed on to us. We were all very subdued and felt very guilty that we had not taken more notice of her podgy weight in the tunic and the slower pace of her walking. She had joined the Dental Corps from the Officers' Mess at another camp and she and her boyfriend from the Centre had not long met so he wasn't the culprit. We offered to go and see Julie but we were ordered not to, and Bill seemed to blame us for failing Julie in some way. The atmosphere at work was most uncomfortable for sometime. Though things eventually quietened down and we heard no more of Julie or her baby, we could only hope they had both happily survived.

Before pantomime season finished the dental officers organised a trip for us all to see *Dick Whittington* at the Derby Theatre. We all looked forward to our outing very much, it would brighten the end of a long, dark winter. Some days before the event I began to feel off-colour, I couldn't stand the sight or smell of food and couldn't think what ailed me. "Don't report sick," they all urged, "You must come to the panto." I kept going as much as I could with various spells in the restroom to cog me along. However, on the great day I felt very ill indeed, Capt. Melvin sent me home to his wife to be looked after until it was time to go to the theatre, then I was to meet the rest of the staff there. I didn't really know how I was going to manage this but I did, and joined the others on the very front row of the stalls, just below the stage. Curtain up and *Dick Whittington* swung into action. The bright lights and the heat got through to me but I hung grimly on and laughed and clapped with the rest, a whole row of khaki-clad figures out for an evening's fun, who was I to spoil their enjoyment, and the show went on. At one point Dick's cat sprang down from the stage and came to rest, of all places, on my lap. He perched there as best he could pawing and rubbing his head close to mine, his great shaggy coat smothering me, much to the amusement of the audience who responded with whistles and clapping and I nearly fainting in the heat and sickness. I was thankful when he leapt back onto the stage and I was free again. I've always regretted that I couldn't then appreciate the fun and make the most of my comical situation. At last the show was over and I staggered out with the rest, but I had come to the end of my tether. "It's no good, Cathie," I said, "I just can't go on to the party or I shall die." Cathie was very good, "I'll take you home," she said and we boarded a bus back to the billet, but I can't remember much about the journey. I presented myself to the house Corporal, "It's sick parade for you in the morning, my girl," she said. Morning duly arrived and I trudged down into camp and into the MI room. The MO called me into her surgery, took one look at me and said, "You know what you've got, don't you Woods?" "Yellow jaundice, Ma'am," I replied, because by now I had noticed a decidedly yellow tinge in the whites of my eyes and skin. "It's a spell in hospital for you, I'm afraid," she said. She detailed a corporal to walk back to the billet with me to collect a small kit, and the army ambulance arrived to take me to the City Hospital. From then on I was out of circulation for three weeks. The hospital was crowded, they put me in a small ward with a woman with pneumonia, who was expecting twins, and a girl of twelve. The doctor and nurse arrived to examine me, he poked, prodded and asked me what job I did. I told him I was a dental clerk/orderly. There was a momentary flicker across their faces as they glanced at each other and he muttered, "Not another one," in an aside to the nurse. After they had gone the pregnant woman said, "That's odd." "What do you mean?" I said. "He's my doctor," she answered. Not comprehending at first and too ill to bother I didn't pursue the matter further. Thinking about it later, I realised her doctor was the gynaecologist, but I wasn't pregnant I thought indignantly. Then enlightenment broke through, the 'Not another one' remark from the gynaecologist made me suddenly realise this was the hospital where Julie came with her baby. They must have thought I was in the same boat coming from the same billet. I was very cross and annoyed about this, but I never saw that doctor again.

For a long while I had to live on tripe and onions and green salads. Friends visited me from the billet and gradually I began to feel better and I was moved to another ward. At last the day came when I was discharged from hospital and I found myself waiting on the side of the road for a bus back to camp with my kit, steel helmet and respirator and, as the fresh air hit me, felt decidedly weak at the knees. However, I was free again and had said that I would rather go home on sick leave than have a spell in a convalescent home, which was perhaps a mistake on my part. Back in camp again and in the CO's office expecting to go back to my billet for the night but not so, the Army had other ideas. "Very good, Woods," she said, "Off you go on seven days' sick leave," handing over my necessary papers. "Have I got to go now, Ma'am?" I exclaimed, "It's late and I'll never get a bus connection from Grantham to take me to Croxton." "Yes, off you go," she said, "You'll manage." Once again I was on my way, I collected my kit from the billet and fled to the station to catch my train. The spring afternoon was turning cold and grey as the train pulled out of the station and its wheels started to beat out a familiar refrain, 'You're going home, you're going home, you're going home'. Drawing into Grantham Station I pulled open the door as the train came to a halt and ran along the platform and out through the ticket barrier, I knew there would be no time to lose if I were to catch the last bus out of town. Down Station Road and on to the Harlaxton Road as the bus came sailing along, luckily the driver saw me and stopped, I dropped into a seat, hot and sticky and decidedly groggy. At last I was at home, Mum and Dad none too pleased at the way I had been turned out to my own devices after such a long stay in hospital. However, next morning I had recovered somewhat and was able to visit Maisie who was in hospital once again. It was lovely to see her, and I was hoping to visit her several times whilst I was at home. Sadly, not to be, next morning I had a raging sore throat and a temperature, so the local doctor was called and I had to stay in bed. Feeling really ill and not well enough to return to camp on the specified date Dad sent a telegram to Company Office to tell them of my plight. The next day, to our great surprise, an army ambulance stopped outside our house and an army doctor and orderly knocked at the door. Dad was out posting, so there was only Mum to cope, she brought them upstairs to me looking a bit flustered in this unexpected situation. The doctor examined me then gave his ultimatum, either I go back with him to hospital or take the train back to camp. Not wanting another spell in hospital I opted for the latter, not in the least feeling like making the effort, but needs must when the devil drives, as they say. Mr. Baggaly, a local farmer, was pressed into service to take me down to the station in his car. Once again on the train, wheels were beating out the refrain, but this time it was, 'You're going back, you're going back, you're going back', and there I was reporting again to the guardroom and soon back in my old billet. On sick parade the next morning, the MO was cross with me for not going to a convalescent home. After an examination she sent me once again on ten days' sick leave, why I had to go back to camp in the first place, I don't know, weird and wonderful are the ways of the Army!

This time I began to feel better, and Maisie was home again, so in spite of my rough time I was back on my feet, painful though it was, as arthritis seemed to have got into my ankles, my weakest point since infancy. Mornings were especially difficult, walking to the bus stop was a slow, painful process, but Cathie was a great help once again, I leaned heavily on her until with exercise the pain wore off, and eventually left me for good.

It was about this time that we met the kindest person during our stay in Derby. We used to meet a certain lady as we took a short cut through a street to the bus stop. She would smile at us and say a few words and eventually invited us to tea one Sunday. We appreciated that very much and enjoyed our cosy visit even though we paid the price of having to go through her family photo albums, accompanied by the family history, all strange and strangers to us. We had hoped to build on the friendship, but time ran out on us. We heard on the grapevine that dental clerk/orderlies were being sent to Cambridge Hospital at Aldershot for courses on administration and dental mechanics, and our time in Derby was drawing to a close. It had been a quiet time as far as the war was concerned, the awful raids on the cities had petered out before we arrived there but for the occasional sneak bomber. Such a one gave us a sharp reminder one morning just before we started out for work. All hell seemed to break loose, the Corporal ushered us all into the small back kitchen reckoned to be the safest place in an air raid and the terrible noise outside seemed to last forever, with shrapnel from the guns behind the house clattering on the window panes. One girl had a great panic attack, screaming for all she was worth and rushing between us all and out of the door, the Corporal rushing after her to bring her back, no easy task. She was oblivious to words, so action took over and the Corporal slapped her sharply on the cheek, she collapsed like a deflated balloon and the emergency was over. The guns stopped, the all-clear was sounded and we breathed again as we set out for the Dental Centre. We never heard where the bombs had fallen, if at all. Our postings came through, Cathie and I were to go to Aldershot. We begged to be posted back to Derby when the course was over, but no one could promise us that. We were sad to be leaving, we had made friends and been happy there, but at least Cathie and I were going together and there's nothing like having a friend beside you when stepping out into the unknown. We packed up our troubles in our old kitbags and tried to smile, it was like leaving home all over again. We humped our kitbags, cases, steel helmets and respirators onto the bus to the station where we caught the train to London.

# 28

# New Friends

Arriving in London, what a nightmare, crowds of people, moving staircases and underground trains, struggling with our gear and trying to find out how to get to Aldershot, the very name putting fear into our hearts. One or two kindly people did help us, one soldier telling us to stay with him and he would see we got on the right train, no signposts or station names to tell us the way. We had gone quite a distance on the clattering tubes when our good Samaritan jumped up in great consternation, we were going in the wrong direction. Off we all got at the next station and the poor lad kindly put us on the right train and at last we arrived at Aldershot. We shouldered our baggage and left the station, military personnel were everywhere. We found a small café close by with a friendly little proprietor, he was used to seeing travel-worn service bods sinking onto his chairs desperate for a cuppa. He went into action immediately bringing us tea and whispering, "Would we like a boiled egg?" I wasn't too keen on eggs but I had one so as not to hurt his feelings. We found our way to the barracks and the ATS Company Office and reported our arrival. Other girls were waiting around to be shown their billets and eventually we came to rest in what had been the married quarters for the soldiers and their families. Four of us occupied the ground floor of one house, Cathie and I sharing the first room on entering the front door. Big Betty and Little Betty shared the inner room, there was a toilet and a kitchen at the back. Other girls lived in the rooms upstairs and there were girls in the houses along the street, all of us on the same course. We settled ourselves in then decided to find the ATS Club, which turned out to be very nice indeed, what a massive place Aldershot seemed to be.

The hospital was large, but we never went inside the main building. Our lecture rooms and laboratories were reached down a side road and here we went every day to be instructed how to do plaster modelling for dentures, bites and try-ins and learning the administration side of running a dental centre. The ATS had to join the army personnel for church parade on Sunday, hundreds of khaki-clad men and women drawn up in ranks on the Square. There, on one of these parades, standing at attention not a stone's throw away from me was a lad who lived next door but one in Croxton. What a coincidence that in all that sea of khaki one should come across the boy next door. We only had time for a quick smile of recognition as we marched off and our paths never crossed again until after the war.

One evening at the ATS Club I was sitting out watching the dancing when a soldier next to me asked if I would like to dance. He was in the Canadian Army, an ordinary, tough-looking soldier, though kindness itself. He apologised for his heavy army boots, which he shouldn't have been wearing for dancing on the beautiful floor, but he seemed to think for once it didn't matter, and for all his heftiness he danced well. He told me his brother had been killed in the Dieppe raid, I felt so sorry for him. After this he would wait each day for me at break time when a group of us would go up to the Club for coffee and it was no time at all before we were all going to the Canadian Club instead. He would wait there for us with a table, no standing in queues with him as an escort, and coffee and doughnuts at the ready. Things we never saw in our canteens were plentiful in the American and Canadian Clubs. We had Naafi, Salvation Army, Church Army, WRVS and other voluntary groups who set up canteens and were very good to the service people away from home but luxuries were in short supply in this country, although the atmosphere in most of them was warm and friendly.

Our course progressed as we worked our way towards exams and spring turned to summer.

Frank and I spent the weekends shopping or walking in the countryside round about. It was very nice having an escort, but he was getting serious and I wasn't so I tried not to encourage him. Big Betty used to tell everyone in the Club that, "He sat looking at Grace with love in his eyes and she was staring out of the windows!" One dull rainy evening a girl from upstairs came down and entertained us with her dance routines, wearing her bra-top and grass skirt, she tapped and twirled around whiling away the hours till bedtime, we had quite a party. At last we were all tucked up in bed and fast asleep and silence reigned along our little street. Suddenly I was woken by a terrible scream like the skirling of Scottish bagpipes away in the heather. Cathie was shouting from her bed by the window, "Grace, Grace, there's a man," her hysterical voice ripped my dreams apart. "There isn't a man," I said woozily, "Go back to sleep, you're dreaming." I turned over and pulled the bedclothes over my head. "There is a man, there is," yelled Cathie, and with that I heard a door click, I sat up, she was right, someone was in the room. I called through to Big Betty in the inner room, "Come quick, Betty, there's a man in here," but she rejected my plea, "I'm not getting out of bed," she said. "Oh, come on, you've got a torch, and I can't get the blackouts up on my own," I pleaded. "Right then," she said grudgingly, "We'll both put our feet on to the floor together." How we were supposed to know when the other's feet touched the floor I didn't know, but we both scrambled out and got the blackout screens up at the windows and switched on the light. Cathie began screaming again and pointing to the floor, there to our horror was a man's pair of trousers and one sock. With a sharp kick I sent them out of sight into the corner and proceeded to try to quieten Cathie, in the end a smart slap on the cheek did the trick. Where had he gone? we wondered. Not far without his trousers, we thought. Little Betty was out of bed by now and joined us, Big Betty volunteered to go down to the Military Police's Office at the bottom of our road and report our predicament. "You stay here," she said, "Get the poker and keep guard until I get back," and pulling her greatcoat over her pyjamas went out into the rainy night.

Cathie had lit a cigarette and sat wide-eyed on her bed, "All I could see were his long, white hands pulling at the blankets," she moaned. The blankets were actually the things that stopped him getting in the bed beside her, we made up our beds sleeping bag fashion, one blanket spread widthwise across the bed under the mattress and the two sides folded across the bed envelope fashion, thus no easy way into bed except to slide down from the pillow.

Back came Betty with two burly policemen, one look at Little Betty and me standing there in our blue and white striped pyjamas holding long pokers was enough to bring a not-too-well-disguised twinkle to their eyes. "Now then, what's been happening here then?" they enquired and Cathie proceeded to tell her tale. We presented them with the trousers and the sock, which for some unknown reason I had picked up and placed neatly on a chair. They examined them and found his army number on the waistband, "Come on then, which one of you knows a Canadian?" was the next question. Accusing eyes turned to me, "I do," I said, "but it wouldn't be him, he wouldn't do such a thing." "Ah," said one redcap, with a knowing wink, "You don't know what these Canadians will get up to," and now there was a decided twinkle in his eye. They searched our rooms and then went upstairs, the girls up there had been thinking we were still partying by the noise we were making, some party!

At last the policemen left taking the trousers and sock with them, "In future put your blackouts up before you go to bed and lock your door," was their parting shot. We tried to settle down to what was left of the night thinking we would never feel safe again. Cathie reported the incident to the Company Commander next morning but all she said was, "Never mind, McKenzie, these things do happen sometimes." Some days later she was called to an identity parade to pick out the offender, she couldn't because she never saw his face clearly, only 'his long, white hands'. Apparently he had entered another girl's room before ours, she had switched on her light and so saw his face and was able to identify him. It seems they caught him that night, two miles away, running towards his own camp in his underpants and one sock, I bet his face was red.

Things settled down and we took our exams and all passed. Our postings came through and I was to go to Knutsford in Cheshire and Cathie to Leicester. "You lucky old thing," I said to Cathie, "That's right near my home." Big Betty heard me and promptly offered to change places as she had been posted to Leicester. We went to Company Office and they agreed on a cross posting so, together once more, Cathie and I took the train to Leicester.

# 29
# Old Friends and Women Dentists

In Leicester I found myself standing in the familiar Guardroom at Glen Parva Barracks where I had started from a little less than a year before. Now I belonged to HQ Company and was given a red band to wear on my shoulder tab. This time I wasn't taken to the spiders but to Aisne block, one of the red brick buildings on the edge of the Square, not far from the main gateway. We were taken into the block and up the stone staircase into our barrack room. We looked aghast at the two lines of beds, head to head, down the whole length of the room separated by tall green lockers, this was the first time we had been housed in a barrack room since training days. We had been spoilt, living out of camp in a house with ATS staff to look after us and weren't looking forward to sharing with so many girls. My bed was fourth in line down the right-hand side of the room and Cathie's at the far end in a corner. We dumped our kit and took stock of our new surroundings, I inspected the front of the girl's locker on one side of me and found her name was Phyllis Latimer, there was also a nice verse stuck on her door, she must be pleasant, I thought, with that sort of poetry on her door. I unpacked my kit and stowed it away and waited expectantly to see what Phyllis was like. She came back from her job in the stores, I thought she seemed very sophisticated and she spoke with a Norfolk drawl. She was friendly, but of course already had a friend further down the room with whom she went out regularly so I didn't get to know her much at first. The girl on the other side of me was a cookhouse orderly called Amy and next to her were two Jewish sisters, who were cooks. The cookhouse staff had to get up very early in the mornings and worked different shifts, which disturbed girls on normal working hours, so it was decided to move Phyllis and me to the far end of the room near Cathie, and I got a corner bed, which suited me well. The other girls called it the

'West End'. Mary made up our foursome along the end wall and we all became great friends. Cathie and I soon settled down in the Dental Centre where there were three surgeries, a waiting room, a plaster room and an office run by a male corporal. A major was in charge of the Centre and two dentist captains, and we all got on very well together. There was a connecting door through to the MI Room was where I first learned to shed my inhibitions. Opposite our surgery windows was the Camp Hospital (the CRS), and surrounding us all a shrubbery of evergreens so we had a nice quiet little corner.

Our patients were primarily the ATS intakes, but at intervals we would get soldiers from outside units. The ones I remember most were the men who had to be made dentally fit before they took part in the ill-fated Arnhem landings. They were grand lads, one or two were detailed to polish our surgery floors, swinging the heavy polishers we called bumpers easily over the large expanse of brown lino. One day they had all gone, and the newsreels at the cinema told us the rest of their story. Some did come back and a welcome-home parade was organised in Wigston for them. One laughingly told us that he was so frightened when he parachuted out of the aircraft his teeth chattered in his pocket. Evidently, before they jumped they were ordered to remove their dentures and put them in their pockets. I've heard this story a good many times since then under different circumstances, but I feel this is the original version.

On Sunday, whenever I could, I would go down to St Thomas's Church on the corner in South Wigston, sometimes Cathie would come with me. After a little while we decided to walk to Wigston Magna and see what the church there was like. It was quite a long walk from the barracks and we were a few minutes late arriving and, to our surprise, the church was full. The churchwarden conducted us to the only two seats left, up at the front. The congregation were singing a hymn and as I knelt down the other occupants of the seat sorted out a book for us, then we rose and joined in the singing. I glanced sideways to see what our companions were like, I met their eyes gazing at me in wonder, and mine registered disbelief for there, standing alongside, was Miss Daft, my old teacher from Croxton Kerrial School. We were wrapped in the warmth of happy reunion, but had to wait until after the service to express our pleasure properly. It was the most friendly congregation I had ever come across on my travels, I think seeing young people in uniform gave them all a surprise and they were like clucking hens round us. Miss Daft and her mother seemed quite proud to know us. They insisted we went home with them and after that it was my custom to visit them for tea most Sundays, when I wasn't on duty or on weekend leave. Afterwards we would go to evensong at the church then back for supper and I would walk back to barracks. Sometimes if some other churchgoing friend was free she would go with me and sample the comforts of open fires and homemade cakes. The Dafts sort of adopted me for the duration. When I was in the CRS with my gastritis attacks they would visit me and bring me little parcels, which I really appreciated.

Rumours of change were circling round us at the Dental Centre, new surgeries were being built in another part of the camp and new officers were expected to fill them. One day we heard that two women dentists had been posted to us. Shock, horror, women dentists! We were adamant we were not going to work with women dentists! The men laughed at us, "Of course you won't, you'll stay with me," said my officer, I didn't quite believe that, one has to obey orders in the Army.

Sure enough, on going back to the Centre one day, I went into the waiting room to put my mug in the cupboard and there was the Major with two women officers, a captain and a lieutenant. He was showing them round, I stopped in my tracks and stood to attention and was properly introduced. One was short and neat and businesslike whilst the other was taller and fair and what I always described as fluffy! They went on their way, I bust myself to tell the others what had happened – it was true – we had women dentists now. We didn't like the idea of having to work for a woman one bit. Nevertheless that was our lot. The men officers were sent over to the new dental centre and the women took over their surgeries, I found myself working alongside the short, dark one, Captain Patricia Burke. At first it was a great disappointment, but I have to admit there was an almost instant rapport between us. She told me that as soon as she saw me the first time she meant having me to work with her. We worked brilliantly together, she was very professional in her approach to her job and very appreciative of my part in the running of the surgery, we became great friends, although we never met other than at work – she being in the Officers' Mess and I in the barrack room. Officers and other ranks weren't encouraged to fraternise. Life took on a very comfortable pattern and I felt that I had reached my natural level and was quite capable and in control of my life. There was a good bus service from Leicester to Croxton so I could get a sleeping-out pass and nip home. Maisie had one or two nasty bouts in hospital and Dad had his usual bronchitis, Mum kept the home fires burning, and Frankie growing up in leaps and bounds.

Great excitement in the camp, one of the Naafi girls was to marry one of our male dental orderlies at St Thomas's Church, Wigston. Vicky, one of our girls, was making her trousseau from parachute silk and we were all contributing to the event. One day, Vicky asked me if she could borrow my case, offering to lend me a certain book as a return favour, I obliged. Meeting her in the corridor the day before the wedding with the case packed a sudden thought struck me. "Goodbye," she called. "I say, Vicky, you aren't running away are you?" I asked. "Of course not," she laughed, "This is my uniform for the cleaners." Oh well, stupid of me, I thought and went on my way.

Next day Alice, the bride, had everything laid on, relations and friends had arrived in Leicester to attend the wedding. Alas, grief and misery, Vicky had run away not only with the trousseau, but the bridegroom as well! The bride was desolate, she was whisked away on compassionate leave and we never saw her face over the Naafi counter again. Neither did I see my case again, Vicky never came back and we never found out what had happened to them all. There was a rumour that the bridegroom had gone home to his mother so whether he ever did marry Vicky we don't know.

In July Dad was finding it increasingly difficult to get leather for his boot repairing and was worried about how to make ends meet. He wrote to the Head Postmaster in Grantham to ask if his part-time duties could be extended or if there was any other job going for which he could apply. The reply to his letter was negative so they still had to struggle on.

Stan was still writing from the Middle East, one brother had joined him there and his eldest brother was a prisoner of war.

*From left to right: Grace Woods, Cathie Mackenzie and Phyllis Latimer.*

# 30

# Bereavement

Maisie's seventeenth birthday was on September 10th. I bought her a necklace of gilt leaves and sent it to her packed in a small denture box. She had grown up to be quite attractive, of average height, plumper than me, with almost-black hair and lovely big brown eyes. She was still helping with the evacuated children at the Red House at Knipton in-between her spells in hospital, which seemed to be happening more frequently.

Regular mail was coming through from West Africa from Tom. Very interesting letters but, of course, censored, so we didn't really know what he was up to out there. He was moved around sometimes and we never knew where he was. But back at base he managed to see some films, and he went to a church service in camp – what he described in his letter as 'the funniest service ever, the native soldiers murdering the hymns and chanting the prayers like parrots, not knowing the meaning of the words!' He didn't seem to be able to come to terms with the native people at all. He wrote to Maisie just before Christmas, saying there was nothing out there like an English Christmas except oranges.

Snow came in December and for me my old complaint, chilblains, no fun at all getting up whilst the stars were still shining and hobbling down to the cookhouse through the snow and ice for breakfast.

Christmas arrived, a cable from Tom to Mum and Dad was happily received. He sent loving wishes and hoped next year he would see us all together again; then we would have a beano.

In barracks we had a wonderful time starting with a fancy dress dance on Christmas Eve. We all decided to hire fancy dress, mine being a Nell Gwynne costume, a lovely dark green crinoline with a little tight bodice, low at the front and back. Cathie lent me a little silver cross to wear to 'fill in a bit'. I wore my hair in ringlets, there was a Madame Pompadour wig I was supposed to wear, but it got too hot and cumbersome. It was lovely getting out of uniform and getting into silk. I had a wonderful time, in fact, we all enjoyed it very much and danced until one o'clock in the morning. Up at 7.30 a.m. to go to breakfast on fried bacon and egg etc., then on church parade. Some of the other girls and I went into the choir. After that a treasure hunt had been organised. We were given a list of things we had to find in the camp. Mavis and I teamed up and spent a hilarious time hunting for a man wearing long woollen underpants. At last a man who had been insisting his were short ones owned up and admitted to wearing long johns! We also found an alarm clock that worked, luckily someone had been given one for Christmas. At last it was dinner time, roast turkey and pork with all the trimmings, potatoes, sprouts etc., Christmas pudding and mince pies. The officers waiting on us and signing our menu cards as a last memento of a wonderful Christmas. After all this we slept for a while then went to a tea dance in the YWCA, but we were too full and tired to dance much. In the evening there was another party where we were all entertained by the officers and, all the time, beer flowed like water for anyone who cared to imbibe, and food, we'd never seen so much for years, four large, square iced cakes, all kinds of savouries and coffee and lemonade. Large decorated Christmas trees were everywhere. A pity children couldn't see them.

On Sunday I went up to the Dafts and on with them to the Stationmaster's house to tea where he persuaded me to try a little rum in my tea, I really didn't like it, but they were all very kind to me and so Christmas 1943 was a very good one for me, but I was wondering all the time how they were faring in Croxton as the old year was drawing to a close.

On New Year's Eve, I received a telegram from Dad saying 'Come at the weekend, Maisie in hospital'. Sudden cold fear, "Why had he sent a telegram?" I felt I should go home right away. I consulted Captain Burke. She said it didn't sound urgent, but why not go to Company Office and see if they would let me go. I lost no time in getting there. The Company Commander said, "Doesn't seem very urgent, Woods." "No, Ma'am," I said, "but with diabetes in one so young one never knows how things will be." "Very well," she said, "I'll give you a forty-eight-hour pass, if you need any more time, give me a ring and I will extend it." Very relieved, I rushed back to the barrack room and packed a small kit and was away to catch the bus from Leicester.

Darkness was closing in as the bus reached Croxton, I arrived in the house just as Mum and Dad were finishing their tea. "What are you doing here?" was their greeting. "I just got worried and thought

I had better come." Apparently, Dad had thought that I hadn't been home recently and it would do Maisie good to see me at the weekend. Slowly I relaxed a little bit but couldn't shake off the dreadful feeling of foreboding which had been with me since receiving the telegram. I had something to eat and before the table was cleared there was a knock at the door. It was the policeman's wife from next door telling us she had received a phone message from the hospital and we were to go there immediately and be prepared to spend the night there. So my gut feeling had been right, we just had time to get into outdoor clothing and rush along to catch the bus for Grantham and the hospital. The bus was late and we waited at the bus stop, the damp and cold wind chilling our bones to match our chilled spirits. We didn't panic, just silently prayed that all would be well, but we feared the worst. At last we were in the hospital waiting room. All seemed emptiness and silence. Fearfully we crouched on the seats and waited and waited, and it seemed to be hours before the Sister put her head round the door and asked Dad to accompany her, Mum and I knew not where. In a few moments he was back, stricken and ashen-faced. "She's gone," he whispered and collapsed beside Mum on the seat. Mum was nigh hysterical with shock, and I could only think of them, I folded my arms around them but nothing could alleviate their terrible grief. The Sister was very kind, she bought us all a cup of tea and eventually took us to see Maisie.

The children's ward was bathed in an eerie blue light and everything was deathly still. Maisie was propped up on her pillows and looked for all the world as though she had just dropped off to sleep. We kissed her dear face and after a few minutes the Sister led us away. They had ordered a taxi to take us home and we all sat in spent silence in the back. As we left, the town bells were ringing the old year out and the new year in. Mrs Jarvis, our neighbour, heard the taxi arrive and was quickly out to meet us, I was so grateful to her for being there. She had kept the fire going and soon had a hot drink for us laced with something potent to revive us a little. Utterly sad we went to bed. 1944 had made a bad start for us.

They brought Maisie home and, like her forebears, she was laid in her coffin in the parlour, looking for all the world like a young bride. Mum and Dad were devastated, but kept up wonderfully for the funeral. I had applied for extra leave and got another ten days, so thankfully I could be with them.

After the funeral I had another sad task to do, one day I walked down to Knipton to see the Matron and collect Maisie's apron and last pay packet. We had to let Tom know in West Africa. Whatever would he do so far away from home? Actually, talking about it years later he

*Tom Woods 1943*

said he had always thought he wouldn't see her alive again after visiting her in hospital on his embarkation leave.

Mrs Durrands collected £12 from the Mothers' Union and others in lieu of flowers and passed it on to Mum and Dad. They decided to donate £10 to Grantham Hospital and the District Nursing Association also received a donation from them.

Everyone concerned had always been very kind to Maisie during her bouts of illness over the past six years.

My leave ended and reluctantly I left Mum and Dad with their sadness. Frankie, who all this time had been staying with the Shipmans, came home and I hoped looking after him would help to fill part of the gap in their lives.

*My sister Masie Alma Woods*

# 31
## The Tide Begins To Turn

Back in barracks, army routine took over and the sad ache had to be pushed deep down inside. The girls rallied round and made up my bed ready for me arriving back. Mum had made me mince pies and Maude a sponge cake. Cathie and Captain Burke were very sympathetic and supportive.

News came through that Captain Burke and Captain Hill were being posted, great consternation! Miss Burke saying that they should post officer and orderly together. On the other hand she said the Major would never part with me, all my own fault for being such a damn good orderly. She thought I would get stripes before the end of the war, but it was still only men who wore those. Periodically, Miss Burke and one or two other

*Me. Private G. Woods*

## The Tide Begins To Turn

people tried to make me put in for a commission but it had never occurred to me that I could be officer material. However, knowing that I would have to give up surgery work and train for something else I didn't feel that I wanted to change my way of life. As it was I received my fair share of salutes! One day going into the office still in my operating gown I found it empty except for a tough-looking ATS training sergeant. "Where's Niblet," she enquired sharply. "Do you mean Corporal Niblet, Sergeant?" I said. She sprang to attention in great consternation, "I'm so sorry, Ma'am!" she exclaimed, "I didn't know you were an officer!" "I'm not," I said. We stared at each other in great confusion. The connecting door to the surgery opened and Miss Burke stood there, she thinking I was getting a ticking off held the door wide saying "I need you here, Grace!" The Sergeant made a hasty exit. "What were you two up to? You'd both got faces as red as turkey cocks," she asked. "She'd just given me a smashing salute," I gasped. She roared with laughter, "You should never have told her you were a private, she would never have guessed." I thought honesty the best policy, I might just have met her on the Square one day!

They left Glen Parva at the beginning of February with many promises of letter writing and keeping in touch.

Army life in Glen Parva carried on much the same as usual. New people were posted to us and others were posted away. Miss Burke returned to the Dental Centre, to our delight, and our working relationship picked up where it left off.

I applied for as many sleeping-out passes, as they would allow so that I could be at home with Mum and Dad as much as possible. They were recovering very slowly from the shock of Maisie's death. Dad still doing his posting, Mum taking over whenever ill health overtook him. She thoroughly enjoying her rounds with the letters.

The Red Cross organised a dance for the forces at Saltby Air Base where the Americans were now in residence. We ATS received an invitation. I decided to go thinking I would be allowed to drop off the truck at Croxton, spend the time with Mum and Dad and be picked up on their way back; it didn't work out like that and I had to go on to the dance. Like all Yank affairs it was pretty luxurious, plenty of food and drinks, though only soft drinks were served, and lots of willing partners, very enjoyable.

September and V-2s, the rocket bombs, were falling on England causing more death and devastation, and our paratroopers had left for the Battle of Arnhem. Some ATS were detailed to go out to the farms for potato picking, gathering in the food was all-important. Mrs Edwards told us she had quite a job to buy potatoes in London, she had to buy cabbage as well before they would let her have any. Dental girls didn't get the chance to go to the farms. It was a full-time job keeping the surgeries going.

The war in Europe was gathering momentum. Dental surgeons were being sent over to the front line to deal with jaw injuries and other new ones took their places.

Occasionally, a girl would get back to her barrack room to find a secret note on her pillow, it told her to report to the cookhouse at a certain time during the night. It meant that the troop train would be passing through Leicester station and our cooks would be meeting it with sandwiches and hot drinks for the soldiers on board for the front or returning to this country for a rest. Nobody talked about it, but turned up at the cookhouse at the appropriate time and gave a hand. Being a dental girl I didn't think I'd ever be called on, so I gave a hint in the right direction that I'd rather like to be involved. It worked and I found a note one day at lunchtime to go that night. It felt strange getting up in the middle of the night, and creeping out of the barrack room and through the camp to the cookhouse. It felt as though I was on a secret mission, which in a way it was. We loaded up a truck with the food containers and huge urns and were on our way into Leicester. The train rushed into the darkened station with a great hissing of steam and ground to a halt. Weary steel-helmeted soldiers lowered the windows and gratefully took the packets of sandwiches we handed in to them. They were Belgians, very quiet, they rewarded us with grateful smiles and we could only wonder where they were going and what their fate would be. The regular cooks told us that when the Yanks came through they would throw out cigarettes, candy and chewing gum by the handful, our own lads would be full of chirpy chit-chat, but our poor Belgians looked tired and exhausted and we felt quite sorry for them.

Mary, my other friend and bed neighbour, was engaged to a captain in the Canadian Army and her wedding day was planned. She invited me and several other friends up to her home in Rochdale for the occasion. We all went up together the day before by train and spent the night in the YWCA hostel in Manchester, quite an experience. Next day we went to the Roman Catholic church in Rochdale for the ceremony. Mary had managed to buy a long white dress and veil, instead of flowers she wore a pair of white dove wings – a symbol of peace. As bride and groom came out of the church we formed a guard of honour, a very romantic couple they made. After a somewhat hilarious reception we caught the train back to barracks. One more colleague married off and due to go overseas to live after the war.

Tom was still writing from West Africa, as he told us, sitting in his tent writing by the light of a hurricane lamp, its only drawback being the fumes it gave out. The moon, he said, as he looked out through the open door was on its back, with a haze round it. He was wondering what omen weatherwise this was, Mum might say rain and wind. Apparently they had been having heavy and terrific thunderstorms, which took everything before them even their tents. He had suffered a bout of malaria and had been sent to convalesce to some place far away from the workshops where the climate was beautiful and the scenery out of this world. Their activities there being horse riding, photography, hill climbing and tea drinking with a bit of dancing thrown in.

The war was going well in the Middle East, in June Rome was captured and on June 6th the Allies landed in Normandy. In the cookhouse at lunch time the news went around that our lads had landed at one of the beachheads. Back in the barrack room a telegram was delivered to Amy, her sudden screams rent the air in painful anguish, "My brother's been killed," she shouted. We rushed to her but not in time to catch her before she fled to the toilets and locked herself in. Her screaming continued, she was past listening to our entreaties to open the door, nothing much could be done. Someone called her officer and her friends were keeping vigil outside the door. I had to get back to the surgery so left those closest to her to deal with the situation. When I returned to the barrack room after work her bed was neatly barracked and she had left for her home up North on compassionate leave. It had brought the consequences of war very much closer to home.

In July a letter from Mrs Edwards, our evacuee's mother, told of the devastation done to London by the V-1 flying bombs. To quote her words: 'I dreaded the nights and it was just as bad during the days! We had to keep stopping work to run onto the stairs supposedly the safest place at our factory. There were deep underground shelters but they were so damp and cold I preferred being above ground. Hundreds of children had left London and the streets were very quiet without them.' I think she was relieved that her four children were safely away in the country.

During this period of time Tom had left West Africa and the 4th Infantry Workshops, WAME, and was now in India. He was suffering at intervals from malaria and his eyes were bad with sun glare, but he was coping well. He had taken his trade tests and was on the way to being a fully qualified electrician. I received a greetings letter-card from him at Christmas telling me to 'have a good time and don't spare the dance floor'. His address now showed he was in South East Asia Command and he had become a member of the special force called the Chindits.

Christmas was here once again, nearly a year since Maisie died, I managed to get leave to be at home with Mum and Dad, but it was a sombre time, thinking of the previous Christmas and the following events.

January 1945 – would this year see the end of the war? It seemed hopeful. For the first time we ATS were issued with khaki eiderdowns, what luxury, we wished they had done it years ago. Now we could dispense with the greatcoat in the bed yet be as warm as toast.

On January 25th I went down to the Orderly Room to fill in my Release Book – the first step towards demobilization.

My friend, and next bed neighbour, Phyllis was now married to an American airman. He was stationed near her home in Norwich and she was married from there. Clothing coupons still a necessity when buying clothes, she had decided to hire her wedding dress, veil and bridesmaids' dresses and very nice they looked too in the photographs. After the honeymoon she came back to Glen Parva hoping that it wouldn't be long before the war was over and she would sail away to her new home in America as a GI bride.

In February I received a letter from Tom's 'boy' who looked after him doing the chores etc. He had seen my photograph near Tom's bed and thought it was a real 'lively' one. Tom had told him about me so he had taken it upon himself to write and tell me Tom's latest address. I wrote back to thank him, according to Tom I committed an almost unforgivable sin! White people did NOT write to non-white people, it undermined the whites' authority and was not done. He gave me a right telling off in his letter and I don't think his boy got off scot-free for doing it either! He did write a second letter though so I think he was hoping for a pen pal! The writing and the grammar were beautiful so I think he must have been quite an educated chap!

I had a letter from Stan Yates in the Middle East saying he hoped to be home soon and thought he would stay at Mrs Stubbs'.

Things were slacking off a bit in the Dental Centre though the ATS intakes were still coming in for treatment. Rumour was going round the camp that a man had been lurking around the place and we were all a bit scared to go about on our own in the dark. He had been reported being in the shrubbery round the hospital and the Dental Centre though we never saw any sign of anyone. One night I was on late duty and was sitting at the office desk taking telephone calls etc., when the connecting door to the MI room opened and footsteps sounded along the corridor. A patient I thought, expecting the office door to open any minute, but no, the measured step continued along the corridor and suddenly the lights were switched off, for a moment I froze, was it the lurking man! Well, I was on duty so it was up to me to find out. I stepped out into the corridor and called out, "Who is there? Will you please put the lights on?" No answer, no lights, silence. Again in my best commanding voice, "Put the lights on." This time they came on immediately, bathing the wide corridor in a dim wartime light, and there on the mat stood the ATS Commanding Officer. "What's your name?" she demanded sharply. "Private Woods, Ma'am," I said. "You don't need the lights on here," she said, "Waste of electricity." "No, Ma'am, it isn't, if we get a casualty coming round here for treatment in the dark they can't find their way to the office, and that could be nasty." She backed off and pulled open the outside door, "Oh very well, Woods, goodnight," and she was gone, and I was left feeling quite pleased with myself! Next morning when Captain Burke came on duty she said with a twinkle in her eye, "I hear you had a visitor last night, Grace!" So I knew the CO had been back to the Officers' Mess and told everyone about the episode.

In April the British Legion held a large rally in the De Montfort Hall in Leicester. Groups of members from a wide area of the country attended including men from Croxton. Dad was there with Reg Sear, George Derby and a few others. I went with a detailed party from Glen Parva. There was a parade of standards, speeches, community singing and the Act of Homage. The addresses given by Lt-Col. Sir Ian Frazer CBE, MP "When they come home". Quite a patriotic and moving occasion. The old soldiers including my own father and friends on their side of the auditorium and we young active-service bods of the present day on our side. After it was all over I dashed outside to find Dad's group and was welcomed literally with open arms. Reg Sears lifting me off my feet in his great strong blacksmith's arms and swinging me round to the amusement of my friends waiting. Having told Tom about this episode in a letter, he replied saying he could just imagine Reg greeting me with 'Well bxxxxx! If it isn't our Gracie!' Then he thought Bolivar (George Darby) would be muttering in his beard, slavering down his pipe stem, making a noise like a thorn bush on fire; I suppose he wasn't far wrong.

In May, the German forces in Italy surrendered, and Rangoon was captured. On May 5th German forces surrendered in Holland, North-West Germany and Denmark. May 9th saw the unconditional surrender of Germany to the Allies ratified in Berlin. It was all over after six long, hard years; great rejoicing everywhere. Some of us went into Leicester. Soldiers in the street were going mad, one grabbed me and danced around kissing me with great abandon, and I must say I really joined in. Bonfires and fireworks in barracks celebrated the occasion and there was much talk of demob.

Still the war went on in the Far East. Tom said the news hadn't made much difference to them out there, they often felt they were the 'Forgotten Army'. They were wrong, of course, at least to their long-suffering families and friends. He said they had no extra time off and no extra beer, but I was to believe him when he said he would make up for it when their fighting came to an end. They were still carrying on under extremely difficult conditions. Uncle Jack, Dad's brother, paid a visit to Croxton about this time with his wife Aunt Georgina. I had never seen him before, he had spent many years in the army in India, but was now living in Warrington. They both seemed larger than life and it was nice to have met them, if only briefly.

Talk of evacuees going home and the likelihood of Frankie leaving Mum and Dad. We couldn't imagine him settling down to city life after his years of freedom in the country. None of us felt like parting with him.

My demob number was 41 and Tom's 50 though he being a regular soldier meant that he would be amongst the last to be demobbed. He kept trying to get leave to the UK but he said his name always seemed to be at the bottom of the list.

# 32

# Homecoming

According to news from home some prisoners of war had returned home, Bron and Eric Bass amongst them and there had been a great welcome-home party. Not long after, several stack yard fires occurred and arson was suspected. Eventually the culprit was caught, an ex-POW had felt badly done to because he had been called up into the forces and farmers, their sons or farm workers had been exempt! No doubt his long stay in a POW camp had given him time to think about this and had turned him bitter and vowing revenge.

Mum and Dad were invited up to Belvoir Castle to a garden party, the young Duke of Rutland, wounded and home on leave, wanted to take the opportunity to meet his tenants. Things had been going downhill at first at Belvoir, the old Duke had died, and the wartime economy had taken its toll. Some people thought the young Duke would give it all up, but he told his tenants that they would get it all going again and that if he couldn't afford to live in the castle he would live in a house halfway up the hill.

Tom was twenty-one on June 23rd, his third birthday overseas. As he told us in a letter it wasn't all a twenty-first birthday should be, but he didn't do too badly in the end. He was on duty in the workshop when his mates turned up with gin and tonics from the Sergeants' Mess, they upturned their toolboxes for seats and proceeded to have a real party. One of the non-drinking boys taking over the responsibility of switching off the generators at the appointed time. So his twenty-first birthday in India was something to remember after all. He had received cards from us all and many friends, but had said to hold his presents over till he got home.

Soon he had moved on from there and letters were scarce for a while, when one did arrive we learnt that he was eighty miles from the nearest town and more of a 'Son of Tarzan' than ever!

He was fed up with monsoons, wet conditions, and the lack of beer, their ration should have been three bottles per man per month, but at that time he hadn't seen any. The flies and mosquitoes swarmed around him in their millions and snakes abounded. Apparently there are 200 different kinds of snakes in India, thirty of which are dangerous. He thought they had twenty-nine of the latter round their camp. He said he was fed up with the native people, mud huts and monkeys!

In July Stanley arrived home and soon made his way to Croxton and Mrs. Stubbs' house, hoping that we could meet up and assess how things were between us. It seemed a long time since we had seen each other and I didn't feel too smitten though there was a sense of excitement about meeting again. Company Office allowed a week's compassionate leave when I explained the situation and I set off to catch the bus from Leicester, only to find they were all on strike. Those of us stranded decided to get a train to Melton Mowbray and take pot luck from there. It wasn't a long journey and I was soon leaving the station and making for Croxton on foot. I had only walked a short distance when along came a car already seemingly overloaded with hitch-hiking service people, but it stopped and the driver offered me a lift. In I got, I found I had to sit on a soldier's knee which proved most uncomfortable as every now and again he pinched my bottom, I was most annoyed and affronted but I had to get home, come what may. Was I thankful when we got to Croxton, I asked to be put down at the Peacock and slammed the door so hard when I got out to show my displeasure, I expect the poor driver thought I was a right ungrateful so-and-so. Still, I was home and there was Stan sprawled out in a chair waiting for me, not looking a lot different from the chap who had gone away two years before. No bells rang for me or flutterings at the sight of him and I knew I had been right not to commit myself to an engagement whilst he was away. We were soon chatting as of old and took walks in the countryside but Stan seemed a bit dull and not overenergetic. After a day or two he admitted to feeling quite ill and looking hard at him I could see the tinge of yellow jaundice through the tan on his face. He got worse and suggested that he should report sick to Saltby Airfield and let them take it from there. No transport around so he decided to walk, I going with him to make sure he was alright and to carry his kit. After a slow uncomfortable journey we arrived at the entrance to the Airfield and it was with a sense of relief I watched him make his way to the Guardroom and medical attention.

Back in camp again friends were waiting around to see me, they made a grab at my left hand but I had to disappoint them, no ring! Sometime later I received a letter from Stan to say he was in Leicester

Hospital and feeling a little better. There I visited him several times until he was fit enough to be moved back to his own base. Gradually the gap between us widened and he disappeared from my life.

On August 6th we heard that the first atomic bomb had been dropped on Hiroshima, sheer devastation, death and destruction, what a terrible weapon.

On August 8th Russia declared war on Japan and on August 9th the second atomic bomb was dropped on Nagasaki. That was that, Tom's war in the Far East was virtually over. On August 14th the Emperor of Japan broadcast the unconditional surrender of his country. On September 5th British Forces re-entered Singapore. VJ day in camp, we all had the day off. We went to bed in the afternoon, to Leicester to the 'flicks' in the evening. After that there was a huge bonfire on the Green with the usual fireworks and celebrations. Letters from Tom saying 'No War' didn't seem 'real' and he was wishing he hadn't signed on as a regular soldier. He said he couldn't make much of a celebration out there, but with a little whisky and gin which appeared out of the blue they managed to get a bit merry, and they got two days off duty. He didn't expect to be home very soon as he would have to stay until others had been repatriated.

Some of the girls from Glen Parva married to overseas serviceman had been demobbed, Mary and Phyllis amongst them.

At home things were brightening up, Mum and Dad had taken Frankie on a day trip to Skegness, but he hadn't enjoyed it very much, though I think he had enjoyed the outing on the whole. I was getting home quite regularly, but the bus journeys were a bit tiring. Sometimes going back on Sunday evenings I found them crowded and sometimes only managed to push on by the skin of my teeth. On one such occasion Mum and I were waiting at the bus stop on the main road, there was a long, long queue and I began to get worried, what would happen if I couldn't get back to barracks? Along came a jeep driven by an army sergeant, he slid to a stop as he saw me and offered me a lift, I hesitated, but Mum said, "Get in, gel," so I did and off we went. "Pull your chin strap down," he said, "and hold on." I did as I was told, we perched there open to the wind and the weather and all the speed limits in the world were broken. We couldn't talk, the wind whipped the words from our mouths and tossed them in the air, never in my life had I travelled so fast. He managed to tell me he was on his way home to see his brother who was on embarkation leave and there was no time to be lost. On the outskirts of Leicester he stopped and said that's where our ways parted! Even then he called two soldiers to him and put me in their charge with instructions to see that I got the right bus out of Leicester to Glen Parva. These boys took me for a cup of tea and true to their word took me through Leicester to the bus stop and I was on my way to camp.

The question of my doing physical training cropped up and I explained about my stiff ankle joints. I was detailed to go on sick parade and consequently the MO sent me for an X-ray to Leicester Hospital. I don't think the powers that be believed me when I said I couldn't stand comfortably on my toes etc., they thought I was 'swinging the lead'. I explained this to the doctors at the hospital and, after examining me and taking X-rays, they gave me a note to take back to camp saying 'this patient is obviously unfit for PT'. So I was never bothered again to go down to the gym for their keep-fit sessions!

Tom had been asking for a long time for a photograph of Mum and Dad and myself all together and at last I was able to persuade them to go down to Grantham with me and have a proper studio one done. It turned out very well and was duly sent to Tom. He reciprocated by sending us a few snaps of himself and his mates, he looked so thin but then he never had been all that robust, 'just like a yard of pump water' was how he described himself. Mail was getting through now without being censored so he could tell us where he was and more details of his life in India. The District Commander came down and presented the medals to all those with three years service up to VE day, I missed mine by a month! The story of my life!

We were all given extra VJ day leave. At home there was a change taking place in the church, after eighteen years as vicar of Croxton and Branston, the Rev. J.H. Evans and his

*Photo sent to Tom.*

wife were leaving the village and the Rev. L. Gerrard Wright and his family were coming to live in the vicarage, he being the former vicar at Woolsthorpe. I was not at home when the changeover took place and my first sight of the new vicar was when my friend Jean's baby was christened in Croxton Church. All the godparents were in uniform, a soldier, an airman, me, an ATS, and his father, a sailor. It was a proud moment for me when I handed Robin Edward over to the Rev. Wright at the font, my first godchild was made 'a member of Christ and a Child of God'. The little service over we all made our way back to the Nook for a small celebration. Later in the week I was still on leave, there was a knock at the door, opening it I found the Rev. Wright on the doorstep. When he saw me he was most taken aback, in fact, you could have knocked him down with the proverbial feather. "So you are Grace," he exclaimed as though he had heard of me and had been wondering what I was like, realising then that I was the godmother at the font on Sunday. From that moment on there was a kind of link between us, and I valued his regard. Unknown to me then, Tom as a young teenager had been rather sweet on his eldest daughter when they lived at Woolsthorpe. By now Tom had moved to Shilling in India Command and things were much easier for the lads out there. He said he felt 100 per cent fitter, the food was better and the climate beautiful and he hoped he would stay there until he was repatriated. He said it was more like a holiday after spending two years talking to monkeys. He hoped to be on his way home in about ten months' time. Repatriation was going well and numbers of lads were leaving for 'Civvy Street'. Croxton people had been very good to him, whenever Mum sent a parcel several people would chip in and send cigarettes, soaps and books and he was always very grateful. Not being a smoker myself I spent my cigarette coupons on him, it sometimes took parcels weeks to reach him, but very rarely were any lost or in bad condition.

Still I was getting quite a few sleeping-out passes and going home to Mum and Dad, often taking a friend with me. Most of them lived too far away from their own homes to get there on a sleeping-out pass. Gladys, whose home was in Bradford, took me home with her for forty-eight hours, which was very nice. At Sunday lunchtime her father went to great lengths to teach me how to make the mustard sauce to go with the real Yorkshire pudding.

At Croxton the local airfields were closing down and the Americans going home, things were gradually getting back to normal. Once again Christmas was approaching and this one seemed as though it would be our last in uniform. One night I was fast asleep in bed, but other girls were in various stages of undress before the lights went out when, according to reports, the door of the barrack room was opened and in walked Santa Claus, red cloak, whiskers and sack complete. I was woken by loud laughter and screams and great excitement, it was like a fox loose in a hen house. He had walked all round the room, "He stopped at your bed for quite a few moments looking at you," they said. Trust me to miss the whole thing, who could it have been, the buzz of excitement went on long after lights out. Just the slightest wondering came to me, had it been our dental officers? but I didn't think so, although they were mad enough for anything. We never did find out, but it had been rather fun, whoever it was never filled our stockings!

Muriel and I managed to get Christmas leave together and I took her home with me. She said she liked staying at our house much better than others she went to! Soon after this, in January, Mum, Dad and Frankie all went down with flu at the same time and there was nothing for it but to get compassionate leave and go home and look after them all.

Tom had left Shilling and was kicking his heels in Calcutta waiting for train reservations to take him to Rachi. He seemed to hate it there and called it a filthy place, it was the third time he had been back and was hoping he wouldn't be there long. Now he had been overseas for three years and four months and expected, all being well, to be home by the end of that year.

My friend Jean's brother, the one she had been worried about when war broke out, had been demobbed from the Navy and was back in his old civilian job.

My demob date was February 28th and I looked forward to it with mixed feelings. I had enjoyed my time in the ATS, had liked my job and made good friends and I knew I would miss them, I began to think how quiet Croxton would seem after the busy service life.

Mum and Dad received a letter from the Government Evacuation Scheme's Billeting Officer asking them if they would be prepared to keep Frankie with them until arrangements could be made to send him home. No doubt about it, they were quite prepared to keep him as long as possible. There was a letter from his mother in London saying everything was getting worse there, hardly any food and the children looking thin and weak through lack of nourishment. She and her husband were still living in City Road, but Lily their daughter was home again with them. No mention of having the boys back, but of course, whilst they were still at that address there was no room for them.

At the Dental Centre a spate of spring cleaning took place, everywhere looked spick and span and immediately the Clerk of Works called in and said the painters and decorators were moving in to redecorate the whole building! They duly arrived and life was chaotic, we had to move out of each of our surgeries whilst they were being painted. At last ours was finished and it looked beautiful, I told Miss Burke I envied her working in it, but she said "Well, I envy you," my demob was due in a week or two's time. Wet paint everywhere and I going in through the door forgot and put my hand flat on the panel! Miss Burke wouldn't let the painters brush it out, "Leave it," she said, " as a memento of you!"

Tom was settled into Rachi, lots of his mates were leaving for demob in the UK, which was very unsettling for him. One of them, at least, arriving home to find his young lady about to marry a Canadian, I fear there were many such situations.

At last my great day arrived. We were to leave early in the morning for the Demobilisation Centre in York. The weather was bitterly cold and grey as we congregated outside the Guardroom for the truck to take us to Leicester Station. Cathie had left a day before for a demob centre in Scotland. Miss Burke amongst others got up to wave us off. We all clambered into the truck with our kit, I tried to see Miss Burke for a last wave, but a large sergeant major stood at the back waving and shouting and shutting out the small group of friends we were leaving behind and the truck pulled out through the barrack gates – we were on our way to Civvy Street. Arriving in York there was snow on the ground and flurries of it in the air. We were directed to a large building where trestle tables stood round the walls and here we passed round each one and handed in our hardware, respirators, steel helmets etc., received our demob papers and money and finally we were free. The men were given a demob suit and a pork pie hat, but we kept our kit. We all assembled in the Naafi for a much needed cup of tea and snack, there was much noise and hilarity. During my final days before demob I had been collecting up redundant shoulder flashes and badges and here was a harvest of them for the asking. I went round all the soldiers in my vicinity and begged their redundant badges, they willingly snipped them off their uniforms soon to be handed in. Later I added them to the ones I already had sewn on my knitted khaki scarf.

Time to catch the train back to Grantham, travelling swiftly through the snow-covered countryside as darkness fell. Somehow I felt vulnerable, I wore a uniform but I didn't belong to the ATS any more, I was a civilian but still wore the uniform, a strange feeling of being in no-man's-land assailed me. I reached Grantham at last and onto the bus for home. It seemed aeons since I had left Glen Parva in the morning and I was cold and stiff as the bus rattled and jolted on the last lap home through complete darkness and the slushy snow. Difficult to see where we were but now we were in Croxton, the bus stopped and I stepped down on to the wet pavement, not a soul about but I was home at last. Mum and Dad waiting to welcome me, a roaring fire and a hot meal; later the luxury of a fire in my bedroom. Yes, it was good to be home. Maybe, one day, four years in khaki would seem like a dream, but what memories I had in store.

# 33

# Civy Street and Monkey Tricks

Gradually I settled down at home, I really missed the company of the girls and the busy surgery life. Letters arrived from those left behind including Mata, (another assistant) and Miss Burke. They rejoiced to tell me that the Major at the Dental Centre had dreamt about me after I left. He said I was kneeling in front of him begging to be allowed to keep my operating gown and he pompously saying to me, "If everyone who left the army wanted to take a gown away with them we should be in a mess." They all thought it 'frightfully funny'. I did go back to see them all but things didn't seem the same there, most of the old faces had gone and new ones had taken over. My hand mark was still on the surgery door and Miss Burke had put in for a posting to the South to be near home.

Tom was still in Rachi, things had slowed down considerably there. He was spending a lot of time going to the cinema and lazing on his bed. He said his mates had found that when they had been on leave in the UK how much slower their actions were. They couldn't hurry or keep up the walking pace of other people, their movements were so much slower. Years in the jungle had taken their toll, it would take a long time for them to get back to normal. He was busy studying for his II Class trade test, not really thinking he would get

*Sgt. Tom Woods.*

through. He had adopted a little monkey. He wrote 'She sat on the corner of my bed watching me write and by the look on her face I could swear she could read.' She loved her bath even the powdering bit afterwards, the powder being half talc and half delousing powder. She loved the other animals in the camp and would ride round on their backs as though she owned the place. She had even managed to open the catch on his cigarette case and he caught her eating his ciggies. He wished he could bring her home with him.

News came out that the Duke of Rutland had become engaged to Miss Anne Cumming-Bell.

In March one of the old village characters passed away, old Mrs. Guy, leaving her husband still living in the cottage on Main Street opposite the Peacock. Both were great supporters of the Chapel. Weekdays would see them going about their little smallholding, she in a man's cap and harding apron and he on two sticks. On Sundays they would pass our house on their way to Chapel to pay their respects to God, a real old country couple, the salt of the earth.

On April 27th 1946 the young Duke of Rutland married Miss Anne Cumming-Bell in London at St Margaret's Church, Westminster. Five hundred or more guests attended the ceremony amongst them many employees and tenants of the Belvoir Estates. Evidently, according to old newspaper cuttings, the hats worn by the guests were something to write home about, flowered and feathered, wide brimmed and small, worn with spring suits and spring coats and floral dresses. The bride looked a dream in silver brocade and an heirloom veil. They went to Portugal for their honeymoon and in June came back and took up residence in Belvoir Castle.

In June all the school children received this message from King George VI:

*June 8th 1946*

Today we celebrate Victory, I send this message to you and all other boys and girls at school. For you have shared in the hardships and dangers of War and you have shared no less in the triumph of the Allied nations. I know you will always feel proud to belong to a country which was capable of such supreme effort; proud too of parents and elder brothers and sisters who by their courage, endurance and enterprise brought Victory.

May these qualities be yours as you grow up and join in the common effort to establish among the nations of the world unity and peace.

**GEORGE RI**

A list of important War dates from September 1st 1939 to September 5th 1945 was on the back entitled 'My Family's Record'.

At home I was having a good rest and rehabilitation period, making the most of the summer weather and freedom. I went down to Chislehurst to stay with Betty and Ernie House. I went on the train to London and found Dick Wright, the Rev. Wright's son, was also travelling on it. He was a great companion. The train was so full we had to travel all the way in the guard's van which was quite fun. He took me for a snack in the restaurant car and handed me safely over to Betty who was waiting for me at Kings Cross; I really appreciated being taken care of! Betty and I had a look round the shops in London, a cup of tea in Lyons Corner House Cafe, then caught the train to Chiselhurst. There we met Ernie and their son Richard who was about six months old and very like a miniature Winston Churchill. One day we went to London again and Tower Pier where we got a boat down to Southend, there we disembarked at the longest pier in the country and boarded the little train which ran along its whole length. Army defences still stood along the shoreline, crumbling concrete and rusty barbed wire, stark reminders of the past war years.

Home again and the serious business of looking for a job began. Miss Burke wrote and said she would be 'furious' if I took any other job than 'Dental' for which I had been trained! Dentists were not all plentiful around home and those who were nearby seemed all fixed up with their own receptionists, and I wasn't really wanting to live away from home again.

Jack Wildman was now demobbed and starting up his old business again, seeming to have plenty of work on hand.

In May a letter from Tom told us that he was well and risen to the rank of Sergeant, and was going around looking like a zebra! His food and accommodation had improved considerably, also his pay and he sounded as though he was enjoying life. He was thinking now about buying a few presents to bring home to us, and telling us about a book he had just read which he was sure Dad and I would enjoy, *Verdict on India* by Beverly Nichols. We never did come across that book, but Tom said it would help us to understand about India in 1943 ready for when he came home and was telling his story. Apparently the blurb on the cover read 'No other book on India has aroused so much controversy'. I wonder what it was all about.

The summer days passed, redecorating my bedroom, keeping Hetty company as she trekked up and down the pastures fetching her cows up for milking from the Branston Lane fields and taking them back again afterwards. Miss Burke had got her compassionate posting and had gone to a small dental centre in Bournemouth, only eight miles from her home. No dental jobs turned up for me locally so I applied for a job in Melton as a clerk and got it. On looking in the Leicester paper that same evening I found an advert for a school dental attendant with the Education Department. "There. That's it," I thought, "that's the job I'm having." So I promptly wrote and cancelled the job in Melton with many apologies for wasting their time and wrote after the one in Leicester. After a while I got notification to go for an interview. Mum went with me on the appointed day, though she and Dad must have felt disappointed that I would be leaving home again, but this is what I had been trained for. It seems there were fifty applicants for the job, ten of us on the short list and they needed two! We all sat outside the boardroom door in the Education Department offices and strangely enough I felt utterly confident. Once again, being 'W' I was last to go in. As the doorman opened the door for each girl he said, hoping to put them at ease, "Don't be afraid there are only five men round the table." As I passed him to enter the room he made the same remark. "Oh dear," I said, "Only five!" Don't think he could make me out! There sat the five, the Chief Medical Officer, a Chief Dental Officer, two other dentists and a clerk. "Good afternoon, Miss Woods," they all chorused. I smiled sweetly round them all and felt their approval. After questioning my abilities they asked me to wait outside with the rest. In no time at all the word came out that I had got the job with one other older person. Outside again, I found Mum standing patiently in the street. She was pleased, I think, though Mum always took everything in her stride and supported me. The Chief MO and DO came out and invited me down to see the main clinic there and then, but I felt I had to say that I was sorry I couldn't, I had already kept Mum waiting for what seemed hours. They were very nice and understood the situation and with much charm and hat raising went on their way. Now it was a question of finding digs. Once again I was lucky, one of the unsuccessful applicants came up to me and said she lived at the YWCA and would take us up there if I wanted to book a room. We were very grateful to her and traipsed up to the Victoria Park area and there met Miss Bowen, the Warden, who after a preliminary chat booked me in and all was set ready for me to take up my duties on August 26th 1946 at 9 a.m. Travelling to Leicester the evening before, I was soon installed in my room at the YWCA, sharing with a girl named Audrey who seemed very nice.

At the main dental clinic I was under the wing of the Chief Dental Officer until he had assessed my abilities, then he handed me over to another clinic attached to a school. Periodically, the dentist and I would visit the schools in the city and inspect the children's teeth, later those needing treatment would be sent an appointment to visit the clinic where their problems would be attended to. Each weekend I would travel home which made a nice break from city life.

Audrey, my room-mate, was having an affair with a married man and left suddenly to go away with him to London, I never saw her again.

My next companion was Mary, who came up from her home in Bristol to teach French at Kibworth Grammar School. We were well suited to share with another teacher from the same school and we became good friends. At last Tom arrived home from India, and how thankful we all were that he had come safely back to us. What a wreck he looked, like a walking skeleton, his thin, yellow-skinned face with its sunken, dark-ringed eyes hidden under his wide-brimmed bush hat. He managed to bring us all presents mine being the promised handbag, soft brown leather with a snakeskin panel inset; I bought a pair of shoes to match, very smart. As his long leave progressed he began to look better but malaria and jaundice dogged him for many years to come. We were all home together for Christmas and all seemed set for a happier 1947.

Deep, deep snow early in the New Year, which lasted off and on well into March. Roads were blocked, but only for one weekend did

*Lizzie Goodall Shipman*

*Me. Grace Woods 1946.*

I have to stay in Leicester because the buses couldn't get through. After that a single track with 'passing places' was dug out, the snow each side being level with the hedgerows. After work, at lunchtime on Saturdays I would catch my bus for home armed with a hot water bottle in a brown carrier bag to keep my knees warm on the long, bumpy journey. It probably seemed foolish to travel when the weather was so bad, but I really enjoyed the journeying, it was quite exciting.

Tom was now at Arborfield in Berkshire and doing a job as a regimental policeman until his course started. At home Mother was having to plod round on foot with the mail, Dad having retired through ill health. She seemed to enjoy the snow, sometimes taking Frankie with her round the Lodges. He tramping gamely along with her though ending up with very chapped legs and knees where his wellies chaffed round the tops.

It was March before the real thaw finally set in, from the bus window I saw roadmen cleaning up the remaining dirty, rock-like snow from the roadsides and green grass was beginning to appear. Housewives were busily cleaning their windows and polishing their door knobs, glad at last to be welcoming spring. The sudden thaw caused a great deal of flooding everywhere. I received a message from Mary in Canada to say that her twins had been born, both girls.

Going to church on Passion Sunday, I remember the huge black clouds racing along before a stormy wind and the bare trees bent before its sweeping fury. The long coarse grass, already flattened and killed by the hard winter, was brown and matted round the old tombstones in the churchyard, the stones themselves leaning drunkenly at an angle, neglected and forlorn in a stormy world. Beneath the shelter of the old stone wall a patch of snowdrops had pushed bravely up through the dark earth. In the field beyond tiny lambs lay beside their large woolly mothers, the eternal promise of rebirth and resurrection. The interior of the church was dim and chilly and only a few people knelt in those century-old pews. It was very quiet except for the voice of the vicar intoning the service and, now and again, a quiet cough from the congregation or the rattle of a windowpane high up in the wall. Outside the world might shake, but here was peace and a great love settled on the heart.

Holy Week passed uneventfully, the weather continued cold and rough. On Good Friday there was the news of the passing of Dick Charity.

On Saturday Tom and I went to Grantham to buy flowers for Maisie's grave and the church decorations. The town was crowded, the price of flowers had actually dropped since the previous week and we bought daffodils at 3s 2d a bunch and half a dozen narcissus at 6s 6d. We had hoped to get lilies but at 4s 2d each they were too expensive. We had to be content with what we had, they were very bright and cheerful. It was great to have the same holidays as the schools and be able to be home for all the festivals, the church was still my first love. The long summer holiday passed and Mary and Joan decided to find a flat and invited me to share with them. We found a very nice one in the Stoneygate area, all of us working about the same hours and the same holidays fitted in very well.

In September Frankie's parents moved into a house in Chingford, Essex, and he had to go home and live with them. Heartaches all round, my mother, especially, was very sad to see him go, and it took Frankie a long time to settle down in his new environment, according to his mother's letters. Every holiday he came back to Croxton and when he left school he was back again and settled down permanently as part of our family.

On October 26th, the first really cold day we had had after a glorious summer, the new War Memorial to Ronnie Winn, the only lad killed in the Second World War from Croxton, was dedicated in church. As my mother and I went up to church a keen wind whipped in from the east and scattered the yellow leaves, picking them up and whirling them into the gutters and shady corners. The sun had set over Lings Hill in a flaming orange ball tingeing the white horses tails in the sky with gold, and finally leaving the whole west a crimson glow. Dusk was falling as people made their way early to church, subdued activity there, the churchwardens were in full force busily showing people to their seats. Men of the British Legion were there, old soldiers of two World Wars. On the north wall, right by our family pew, was the War Memorial of the First World War when sixteen men from the village had died in battle. Beneath this hung a Union Jack veiling a small plaque to Ronald Arthur Winn. Everyone settled into their seats, by now the Duke of Rutland had arrived and was sitting in the front pew, and behind him the Commanding Officer of Spitalgate aerodrome. The bells stopped ringing, Eric took his place at the organ and the familiar Voluntary filled the church. The choir and clergy entered and with a great deal of rustling and coughing the congregation rose to their feet and the service began. The 'National Anthem' rang out filling the building and overflowing into the darkening world outside. After a hymn and lessons, one read by the Duke and one by the CO, the former made his way, accompanied by the clergy and the President of the British Legion, bearing a wreath to the Memorial. The Duke removed the flag and the tablet was unveiled and dedicated to the glory of God and in memory of Ronald Arthur Winn, the wreath was laid and the stirring notes of the Last Post rang out. The service was over, it had stirred the hearts and the memories of we who had known Ronnie and, like the other old soldiers, 'We will remember them!'

The Sunday after – not so many people in church, just the faithful few. The wreath of chrysanthemums still hung by the new memorial, beginning to look a little limp with one or two deep red petals from the ledge above making a splash of colour amongst their white blooms. Like drops of blood, I thought, the blood of people of many nations, friends and foe alike, all somebody's loved ones, all mourned by someone, all died – for what?

Letters were arriving from Frankie to Mum and Dad, he seemed to have settled down but said he kept thinking about them all the time and couldn't wait for the Christmas holidays. His Mum said he was crossing off the days on the calendar.

My friend Phyllis, the GI bride, wrote and told me she had arrived in the USA with her baby son Stephen and had found things very much to her liking. Robert, her husband, and all his relations and friends had done everything in their power to welcome her into her new family and new country.

Sadly Joan's mother died and she went home to live with her father. About the same time Mary was offered a teaching post at Bordeaux University. The flat was too expensive to keep on my own so I had to start looking for other accommodation. I spent some time sharing with another teacher, but finally decided to go into digs. I found a very nice home with a single lady, a doctor's daughter of the old school. She already had a domestic science teacher living with her, who seemed to find a lot of things 'most odd'. It was very comfortable, but I still continued to go home for weekends, going back to Leicester after church on Sunday evenings.

For a few weeks before Christmas a German prisoner of war had been attending evensong regularly, sometimes with friends, more often alone. My mother told me he was very friendly with Maud and used to visit the family and go out to the Peacock with them on Saturday evenings. At Christmas he was in church again, a really devout Christian, but nobody had ever bothered speaking to him or made him welcome, only at the Inn was he accepted. My conscience pricked me, was I a real Christian or just pretend? The Sunday after Christmas I made up my mind that I would speak to him, why me, why wouldn't an older member of the congregation accept him into the fold? My fear of getting involved and the possible consequences still persisted but it was no good, I just couldn't sing the Christmas Carols and parrot 'Peace on Earth' or kneel down and say glibly ' Our Father', and deny a lonely prisoner a cheery word in the Season of Goodwill! After the service I said to Hetty, "Stay with me, I'm going to speak to Georg," for I had found out his name from Maud. As we reached the gate at the same time, I asked him if he had had a nice Christmas. Surprised hesitancy on his part as he said he had. We all walked down the hill together until he crossed over to Maud's house in the alley. That was that, I wondered if he had appreciated my friendliness or if he thought I was a forward creature! Back to Leicester on the bus and a week of busyness at the clinics then back to Croxton for the weekend. Church time and I set off with Mum who disapproved of my actions, German POWs weren't welcomed by the older people remembering the First World War and the atrocities in the Second. Found him waiting for me on the hill, could he speak with me a moment? I stayed with him, he wanted to know if my church's priest and congregation would help him financially to send bibles back to Germany for which he had been busy collecting for that purpose, the bibles and religious books there had all been burnt at Hitler's decree. I said I would ask round and let him know the next Sunday, I knew in my heart of hearts nobody would be interested. Waylaying the vicar, I put my request to him, "No," he said, "couldn't possibly do that, out of the question." Quite a rebuff but no more than I had expected, I felt very ashamed of my church then, I decided I would help by myself. Meeting him the next Sunday I gave him the verdict and made my offer. He wouldn't accept it, of course, and said he would manage by himself, he made a bit of money from mending wirelesses. Eventually he managed to parcel all the bibles and get them over to his hometown where his friend was a pastor there. Receiving them with gratitude he said he would wait until Georg was repatriated before handing them over to the congregation. So inevitably we became friends, much to Mum and Dad's dismay and a few raised eyebrows in the village. At weekends we walked and found spots in which to shelter, my parents wouldn't have him in the house, but one or two friends took pity on us and invited us in. It wasn't easy for me, I didn't feel comfortable walking out with a POW but Georg was such a good man and a total Christian, we were both in a situation from which we couldn't back out, and we grew closer as time went on. He was in a camp at Allington and would walk over from there every Sunday to see me and go to church. He would go to Maud's house to eat and there he would shave twice daily, she used to say "My guy, I wish I had a man who would shave twice a day for me!" She would call him her 'young owl', which amused him greatly. After a while he was transferred to Saltby camp, which made things a bit easier, but just before Easter word came out that they were going home. By now Mum and Dad were letting him into the house and, against their will, liked him very much. On Easter morning he arrived for the early service and I was a bit worried in case the vicar refused to let him take part, but Georg had no such qualms. He was a Lutheran and said their church was in communion with ours, so for the first time we sat together for a service and walked to the altar to receive the bread and wine. All was well though I felt relieved when we returned safely to our seats.

Not long after he was moved to Leicester ready for repatriation to Germany. We met for the last time and walked and talked, arriving back at our front door just before midnight, and as the church clock struck the hour we said our goodbyes, and before it had stopped he had gone. As he had planned we parted neither yesterday, nor today, nor tomorrow, a great romantic was Georg. He disappeared into the darkness along the street, I knew I would miss him a lot, but amongst the feelings of sadness and loss was the slightest feeling of relief, it hadn't been a comfortable time for either of us, and I'm sure Mum and Dad were relieved to see him go. Letters passed between us frequently, sometimes two a day from Georg. We were unofficially engaged and he kept asking me to get a visa and the necessary papers to go over there and marry him but I delayed and hung back, I could never see myself happily living in Germany. He didn't seem to want to leave his parents again and come over here after being away from them so long.

On my birthday I received a large photo from him to which was pinned a rose and a lock of his hair. Dottie, my landlady, and the domestic science teacher oozed envy and admiration as I opened my romantic package. Eventually, I decided to leave Leicester and come home for a quiet time in Croxton to sort myself out. I felt that if he really wanted me he would come over here to live, and if I really wanted him I would cheerfully live over there. In the end he decided we had best let go. I felt devastated at the time and thought the sun would never shine again or the flowers regain their colour, but I knew it was for the best. Eventually he met someone else and, I hope, lived happily ever after.

After the split from Georg friends invited me to go with them on holiday to Wales thinking it would do me good to get away for a while. We had a

*Annie Woods (Mum)*

lovely holiday in Llandudno, and it did much to cheer me up. We climbed the Great Ormes on the Sunday morning. Sheep grazed on the slopes and, far below on the still sea, a crowd of chittering gulls feasted on an unwary shoal of fish; and from the tiny church of St Tudno we could hear the congregation singing the first hymn, peace reigned. Like the apostles I didn't want to come down from the mountain.

Home again and Mary, with whom I had shared a flat in Leicester, was due home from France for the summer holidays and her mother wrote and invited

*Dad. Harry Woods*

me to go down to stay with them in Bristol. Mary's sister Eleanor was now teaching at Kibworth Grammar School and was breaking up for the holidays so I travelled down with her. They were a lovely family and made me very welcome. Mary showed me round Bristol University where she had been a student. We visited the Suspension Bridge and gazed across the city to the Cabot Tower. We walked over the common and looked round the zoo, I very much appreciated their kindness and hospitality. So the summer passed and I began to perk up and look once again to the future.

# Part IV

# Manor House Days

# Part IV

## Manor House Days

# 34

# Lord of the Ruin

In 1948 Allington, like many other small villages, was slowly getting back to its peacetime quietness. During the war American forces had been stationed there and the village hall turned into a Naafi 'for the use of'. Land Army girls had been billeted in a hostel along Bottesford Lane and, after them, displaced persons were housed there. A prisoner of war camp was built on the outskirts of the village where German and Italian soldiers were held captive for the duration. Allington must indeed have been a lively place.

Small farms abounded and cows were driven through the village twice a day from the fields for the milking. Little stone cottages snuggled round the Green where farm implements were parked and goats and geese enjoyed their freedom.

The Welby Arms had settled down with its local customers, one could hardly tell there had been a war on, but in some ways life would never be the same again. The Welby family, the old squirearchy of the village, had gone; the hall and the grounds which had been used as an American hospital during the war were empty and the sale about to take place. Bert Jackson had bought part of the gardens turning the Old Dovecote into a house for his family and to set up his market gardening business.

The rectory along Bottesford Lane had long since been sold to a private buyer, the incumbent of the parish, the Rev Spreadbury, living in the rectory at Sedgebrook whose church he also served.

Strangely Allington had two small churches. St James's tucked away in the centre of the village and now unused, plans being afoot to have it demolished and Holy Trinity, almost its twin and still in use, was close to the hall and approached from Bottesford Lane by a pretty drive. Going up on the left-hand side of this drive and separated by a high hedge was what the Welbys called the rhubarb gardens, though the rhubarb had disappeared long ago.

Opposite the church gate stood the Old Manor House, built around 1660, now empty and almost derelict. Its twin Dutch gables and ironstone walls a sorry sight, covered in ivy, saplings growing out of the walls, windows broken, many bricked up since the window tax was imposed.

The front garden was a mass of brambles, ash and elder saplings, weeds growing all around higher than the doors and windows. The back garden was being cultivated by a farmer for growing turnips. The outbuildings, paddock and roadside orchard rented by another farmer for his poultry and livestock. Thus Herbert Palin found things on his visit to Allington to view the hall before the sale.

The Old Manor House drew his attention and he moved in for a closer inspection. Making his way round the back he found the dairy window and made an easy entry. Sheer devastation met his eye, an accumulation of dirt and rubble knee high on the floors, thick cobwebs festooning everything, rushes and loose plaster hanging from walls and ceilings. Pigeon dirt inches thick in the attics where birds roosted at night and rats scuttled freely around. All this he saw with one eye whilst the other registered the good parts. The rooms well proportioned, a beautiful 'dog-leg' staircase in oak and pine, though covered now in thick dark paint and cobwebs. He could see nothing that hard work and 'know how' couldn't put right and his brain started ticking. Several trips back to see it over a period of months, thinking, brooding and working out, to take it or not to take it, that was the question. Finally, in heavy snow a chimney collapsed and fell through the roof and that settled it, now or never. The purchasing process was set in motion and the ruin was his after six heart-searching months. He applied to the county council for a wind and weather grant for the work to be done to keep out the rain and cold, enough money was granted to help him make a start and the mammoth task of restoration began. During the war after D-Day Herbert had been stationed in Holland and billeted with a family who were cabinet makers and wood carvers. Having done his apprenticeship in the trade he was very interested in their way of life and the idea of returning to England and setting up his own business took root. On demobilisation he left his home in Liverpool to join his brother, Jim, in his music business in Grantham, modernising old pianos, which Jim bought in and then sold in his shop. He bought a small row of cottages in Grantham, living in one and renting out the others, bringing his mother down to live with him.

After buying the Old Manor House all his spare time was taken in getting part of it ready to move into, chopping down the vegetation and clearing the ivy from the walls to make proper access into the house. One weekend the place nearly went up in flames. Whilst working there on the Saturday he had burned an old mattress in one of the large fireplaces upstairs. On leaving for home all was seemingly well, the fire out. However, deciding to look in again on the Sunday he found the floor of the passage very hot to his feet. Hastily investigating he found to his horror that some of the joists had ignited and were smouldering away under the plaster. He quickly dampened it all down and saved the situation, thanking the good Lord for prompting him to look in on the Sunday, something he seldom did at that time.

At last a couple of rooms were made habitable. The dining room, where he had his workbench along one wall and a bedroom upstairs divided by a curtain, which he and his mother shared. She, poor soul, suffered greatly from asthma and must have found it very uncomfortable during the first few months. After emptiness and desolation for over eighty years the Old Manor House was occupied once again.

It took another year or two to acquire the paddocks, orchard and outbuildings, but eventually they became part and parcel of the estate. The old stables and cowshed became a workshop and storeroom with the loft above making a useful studio. In other buildings chickens were housed and the orchard on the roadside produced apples with old names such as Beauty of Bath, Keswick, Bramley and Peasgood Nonsuch. Damsons and peas were also there in abundance and in the middle of it all a deep well. There were many wells in Allington, one outside the back door of the Manor was thirty feet deep and had an old iron pump with which the household water was drawn. Herbert once pumped this well dry, and lashing two long ladders together descended into its depths. To his surprise going out in the direction of Belvoir Castle was a tunnel, beautifully constructed of brick and high enough for him to walk along. He was very intrigued but realising he was there on his own he felt it wasn't wise for him to go too far along, but to try another time when someone was with him and make a proper investigation.

As yet there was no mains water at the Manor, nor a sewage system. Herbert sorted the water problem by placing an electric pump in the cellar and pumping the water from the well outside to a large tank in the roof. After doing the plumbing in the house the water was then piped to the newly installed bathroom and kitchen taps. Drains were just soakaways. There was a primitive stone sink in the kitchen where one simply emptied the water into it and it ran through a hole in the wall down onto the cellar floor into a specially constructed channel, through another hole in the wall and out into the farmer's field next door. Where to then, it was anybody's guess, but it all worked very well. Eventually Herbert dug his own drains when the house was connected to the mains water supply. The toilet was a chemical Elson housed in a cubbyhole up the back stairs, emptied regularly into a pit in the garden.

Electricity had reached Allington, but of course wasn't installed in the Manor, but there was a pole right outside the backdoor so it was no problem to connect it to the house. Herbert employed a qualified electrician to do this job and lights and power were installed, gradually things were beginning to take shape. Another bedroom was restored; Herbert put in a new ceiling and opened up the end window looking towards the village. The floor was the old Lincolnshire plaster full of dust and cow hairs. There was a wide open hearth with a fire stone surround, buried beneath a thick coating of black tar, with a fixed mantelpiece covered with the tattered remains of red, tasselled material. He dismantled this and after much hard work removed the tar to reveal the moulded fire stone. The chimney being chock-a-block full of rooks' nests had to be cleared out, but at last all was finished and a fine room had emerged from chaos.

Herbert had made a friend of Alexis Buhryn, one of the displaced persons living at the hostel along the lane. It was now being closed down and Alexis didn't want to move away, so Herbert and his mother offered him a roof over his head if he decorated one of the other bedrooms for himself, which he did and moved in.

The drawing room was in a terrible state. A huge hole in the ceiling where one could look up through the next two floors to the sky, a staggering job for Herbert to tackle. After weeks of sheer graft the walls were rebuilt and the ceiling repaired.

He opened up the end window which had been built up during the glass tax years and let in the light, with the two other windows reglazed this task was almost finished. There was an open hearth behind the small grey marble fireplace which had been placed inside, but Herbert decided to leave that for now and to make things easier he sealed this up and installed an electric fire. The decorating done and furniture installed, all was completed to his satisfaction. His mother made curtains from some old linen bed sheets, dying them cream. Household fabrics and building materials still being on dockets and coupons, it was by no means easy to restore and furnish a large house in these early post-war years.

Herbert made the end room on the south-west corner of the house next to the kitchen into a garage, fitting double doors where a window and stone work had crumbled away, making room to get his small van inside.

On the inside wall of this room was a large open hearth housing five bake ovens at different levels, a very interesting feature, but the walls were crumbling badly and the fireplace arch sagging. So to avert further disaster Herbert bricked up the opening, hoping to reopen when the house was finished. He concreted a large area in front of the garage and leading to the back door and things began to look more civilised. He turned the back garden into three large vegetable plots with an area for soft fruit bushes and planted a new orchard of fruit trees at the bottom.

Over the brick walls surrounding the gardens one could look westwards over the Vale of Belvoir to the distant castle on the hill and see the trains running through the countryside between Grantham and Nottingham, stopping at the little wayside station at Sedgebrook. The other side looked across a small field to the village green with its stone market cross, the Welby Arms and the post office, a truly rural setting for a Liverpudlian to put down his roots.

# 35

## Work and Play

Not until coming to Grantham had Herbert ever danced, but friends introduced him to old tyme dancing and he soon became an enthusiastic member of the club. He started teaching old tyme dancing through the education department in Allington village hall, one evening a week. The classes proved a great success and the village people supported them with great enjoyment. Word got around and Marston people asked if he would get a class going there, so his social life expanded rapidly. His brother owned a music centre and amplifiers, which he hired out to people for their various entertainments and fund-raising efforts. Herbert, being his disc jockey, would transport the equipment round the dances and garden fetes and so became an experienced master of ceremonies.

His business of modernising pianos was beginning to take off and his local jobs including making a set of tables for the Blue Horse Inn at Ponton, his first large assignment. Jim had opened another music shop in the market place in Grantham and was opening up a café above it, Herbert doing the fittings. The dream he had dreamed during his war service had become a reality. The lad from Anfield had become, so to speak, 'Lord of the Manor'. Sometimes he would wonder, "How did I get here? What am I doing here?" What strange twist of fate had brought him to Allington?

# 36

## The Music Man

Life at Miller's Dental Surgery in Church Trees was pretty hectic, everyone taking advantage of the free dental treatment on the National Health Service, but I settled down very well.

In Croxton I took up one or two strings I had dropped when going into the ATS, had weekends with friends and time passed pleasantly enough. Now I had accepted the fact that there were no such things as soulmates, and my faith had grown a little dim. My feet were firmly on the ground and the future looked very ordinary indeed. No more was I prepared to rush in where angels feared to tread!

In April 1950 the Rev. Gerrard Wright left Croxton for a Church in Chichester and the Rev. Fred Tetley took over Branston and Croxton parishes and moved into the vicarage at Croxton.

At the garden fete in June I helped just like old times. Friends came from Leicester to support it and enjoyed their visit very much. We made £101. 5s. 0d., an excellent result. For part of my holiday I spent some time with Cousin Freda at her farm near Spalding.

Mary, my Bristol friend, married Robert, one of her French students, who after a short honeymoon took up a teaching post in Magazan, French Morocco. Mary had to stay behind because of teaching commitments at her school, but after a time of anxious waiting she was given permission to leave at half-term and was soon speeding on her way to him, and they settled down happily together.

Friends seemed to be scattered all over the world and letters came from its four corners.

Christmas was coming round and at a meeting of the PCC held at the vicarage it was decided to hold a party for all church members and their families in January. The members of the Sunday school having a tea in the Stute in the afternoon followed by a social for everyone in the evening. The vicar invited me to 'grace the occasion'; I wasn't sure what this entailed. "Just play hostess and so on," he said.

It turned out that I was expected to arrange the programme of entertainment. Sorting out games to play, singers to sing and the dancing, I came to the conclusion that I would need music; where on earth did one find music? I hadn't a clue. Tom came to my rescue, he knew someone through Jack Wildman who hired out records and amplifiers for such occasions and he would see to the booking for the evening. I was only too happy to leave it in his hands.

Tom was out of the forces now and trying to settle down again with Jack, opening an electrical side to his carpentry business.

Christmas passed and the party day arrived, I keeping my fingers crossed that everything would go according to plan. The children's tea party in the afternoon was great fun. I took little Andrew Poole along with me and he was such a good little boy, enjoying every minute of this noisy affair.

This part of the proceedings over, the Stute was cleared up and prepared for the evening party. I went home to check up on my programme and relax for a while. Down at the Stute once more I found the refreshment ladies laying out the food in the billiard room, everything looked set for a great evening.

Going into the hall itself I spied the music man setting up his record player, large speakers already in place on the walls. For a moment or two I stood watching him and had the strongest feeling in my mind that he was the man I was going to marry! "Oh no," I thought, "No, he's not tall enough, not at all my type! Well here goes, must go over and welcome him and discuss the programme." He looked up at me and smiled broadly, white teeth shining and brown eyes friendly and we slid into an easy partnership which bode well for a great evening of enjoyment for everyone. The Stute filled up with people anticipating a good night out; my music man announced the first dance and taking me into his arms swept me onto the floor. Games and entertainment followed, he made an excellent master of ceremonies. What a stroke of luck that Tom had known about this man and his music set-up. "What's his name?" I asked Tom. "I was told at the shop to ask for a Mr Herbert," he said. My heart sank, perhaps that was his surname, not tall enough and his name is Herbert, just my luck! As we danced he told me that he was restoring a cottage in Allington, that his mother lived with him and usually accompanied him on these do's, but this evening was suffering from asthma and hadn't felt well enough to come.

The party ended at midnight and the Stute slowly emptied leaving Mr Herbert to take down his speakers and carry everything out to his van, whilst Mrs Wells waited to lock up. I stayed with her feeling a bit responsible, also I felt a bit cross that no one had stayed to help him carry out his equipment. I gave him a hand as much as I could and we soon had it all packed in his little van. Mrs Wells locked up and went home.

Brilliant moonlight lit everywhere like day and hoar frost glittered on the ground and roof tops. Mr Herbert had parked his van in the farmyard opposite the Stute, a funny little 'Bubby Hutch' he had made himself. He said goodnight and got into the driving seat, switched on, nothing happened except a splutter or two. He tried again, nothing! "Er, would you mind giving me a push?" he said. I obliged, we manoeuvred it through the gate facing down towards the Peacock. I pushed and without more ado the engine burst into life.

"Get in," he said, "I'll give you a lift home." He drove up the school lane, at the top I told him to set me down, "It's not far to my home," I said. Our front door had proved too handy in the past for would-be suitors, there was plenty of time for Mr Herbert to find his way there!

The weekend passed, as all weekends do, and Monday came with its full quota of patients. I've always liked Mondays, a new start to a new week and who knows what it will bring!

As I was cleaning up the surgery after the morning session the phone rang, "Could I speak to Miss Grace, please?" The voice at the other end of the phone was light and hesitant. I knew at once it was Mr Herbert. "Sorry," I answered, "There's no Miss Grace here, this is Miss Woods speaking," but of course I giggled and he immediately knew who it was. He had heard people calling me Grace at the party and had rung Jack Wildman to find out where I worked and so managed to get my phone number. He invited me to go with him to the cinema at the weekend but I had arranged to go to Leicester so couldn't accept. We arranged to meet the following week. On the appointed evening I caught the bus into Grantham and met him at the top of the bus station outside the Library. We went to the theatre in George Street to see the play *While Parents Sleep* and he drove me home after in his little Bubby Hutch. That first date led to further meetings and we visited the cinema or theatre every weekend.

He was still telling me that he was restoring an old cottage in Allington and I had no cause to doubt him until a farmer from there came in for dental treatment and I quizzed him a bit. He was over the moon with surprise and delight. "Don't tell me you're going out with Herbert," he cried, "Couldn't be better, couldn't be better," slapping his thighs enthusiastically as he sat in the dental chair. Tentatively I queried the cottage restoration, 'Ha ha ha, some cottage," laughed my patient, but wouldn't enlighten me further.

There was to be a dance at the village hall and Herbert invited

*Grace Woods Backyards of 40.*

me to go with him, he would pick me up from the surgery after work, I could have a meal at his place and go on from there. At last I was to see where he lived and meet his Mother.

It was darkish as we drove to Allington with fitful moonlight appearing now and again between heavy clouds. The house rose up dark and mysterious as we turned into the drive, a man was waiting there to speak to him, "Won't be a moment," he said as he got out of the van and disappeared into the darkness. There I sat waiting patiently without a clue to my surroundings, when suddenly a light was switched on behind me and a thin asthmatic voice called out, "What's he thinking about leaving you out there on a night like this." A figure approached and pulled open the door, "Come in to the warmth," and I was escorted into the house by his mother, and there I was on my first visit to the Old Manor House being seated at the table and plied with huge plateful of sausage and chips.

Before going to the dance Herbert thought he had better show me the part of the house which had been restored. We passed through the large, flagged entrance hall where rushes hung down from great holes in the ceiling and there were gaping holes in the end walls where fireplaces should have been. The room itself being full of pianos awaiting their turn in the workshop for modernisation.

Through to the drawing room, he opened the door, what a difference from all the dilapidations all around us. Three large windows now looking out on to the dark night, pink walls, cream paintwork, large easy chairs, all comfortable with no hint of the amount of work put into it to make it so.

The front staircase was in the same sorry state as the hall, broken plaster, rushes hanging down everywhere, the woodwork covered in old paint and years of dust and grime, and cobwebs everywhere. The two windows on the end wall were fitted with iron bars, no doubt telling of more lawless days in the past.

By now two other couples had arrived and we all went down to the village hall together. There we found the members and friends of Herbert's Allington old tyme dancing class waiting to start proceedings, a roaring fire burning in the hearth giving the room a cosy, homely feeling. It was a happy, friendly occasion and the start of a lifetime of happy occasions for both of us.

## 37

## Future Together

For several weeks I went with Herbert and his mother to the Harrowby Hut Hops where Mr and Mrs Page taught old tyme dancing and where Herbert learned the new ones to take back to his classes at Allington and Marston.

Some weekends I spent at Allington giving a hand with any restoration jobs which happened to be in progress.

We visited the tulip fields at Spalding, acres and acres of beautiful blooms all soon to have their heads picked off, only the bulbs being needed for marketing. The flower heads were used to decorate the floats every year at the Tulip Festival in town. We heard later that Cousin Freda's son Philip was born on the day we were there. Just a piece of family history, Spalding being my father's hometown.

Tom was busy installing electricity in our house in Croxton, I paying for the materials and he giving his labour free so that Mum and Dad wouldn't be worried about the cost in any way. In June the meter was installed, now we could get light by the flick of a switch and candles and lamps became a thing of the past.

Allington Hall, which had stood empty and neglected since the war, was auctioned at the George Hotel, Grantham. Herbert and I went to watch the proceedings but though there were a lot of people there it was withdrawn at £950.

We travelled with a busload of people from Croxton to the Festival of Britain in London. It was a vast area of trade stands etc., the showpiece being the Skylon. This was a vertical feature made of steel and aluminium, it stood about 300 feet tall and was suspended on steel wires. A comment made at the time about it was 'A tall thin structure with no visible means of support, rather like the British economy'.

Croxton church held its garden fete in June in the vicarage garden. Molly Shipman and I put on an exhibition of old Croxton artefacts and bric-a-brac. People were very good at lending their treasures and we put on a good show in one of the vicarage rooms. We both dressed in Victorian clothes kindly lent by Mrs Shipman and a lovely shawl loaned by Harry Farnsworth. Our photograph appeared in the Grantham Journal buying a buttonhole from the three flower girls Linda Ward, Mary Lambert and Pamela Crick. We made £78 profit from the event, quite a good effort so we thought.

Now it was the season of garden fetes with Herbert toting his music round most of the local villages at weekends, I going with him, each fete being much the same as the last one.

In July we took Mum

*The Skylon 1951*

and Dad over to the Manor for the first time. They weren't greatly impressed, Mum thinking it was so big she would get lost, and saying, "Oh dear, what a lot of work to be done." Amongst all the comings and goings, not to mention the work in the workshop, the restoration of the house continued.

The huge open fireplace in the kitchen was partly built up to provide a small 'walk-in' cupboard for buckets and brooms, the rest arched over a concrete platform built to support a small iron stove. One could still stand inside the vast chimney where in times past little boys would have been sent up to sweep down the soot. On the left-hand side of this cupboard was a bricked-up opening which, we felt, was an old bread oven, and which Herbert promised himself that, one day when he had time, he would open up. The floor of the kitchen was half old and worn red bricks, the other half flagstones and just inside the back door a large millstone had been let into the floor. Three worn steps led out of the kitchen up to the dairy, which Herbert had already restored. It was a lovely old place with beamed ceilings, and the old timbers visible in the lath and plaster walls. Old shelving and a stone bench ran along one wall underneath which were arched alcoves. Limewashed throughout it was a very useful storeroom.

In July we became engaged only after a great deal of thought on my part. Herbert had been married before and was a divorcee and it took me some time to come to terms with that. However, I did really feel that our futures lay together and only good would come from our marriage so eventually I said 'Yes'. He gave me a ring with three diamonds and I gave him a pair of gold cuff links with his initials and the date of our engagement.

My parents weren't too pleased about the situation, especially when I told them we probably wouldn't be married in Croxton church, the stumbling block which took the gilt off the gingerbread. However, once committed I just hoped as time went by things would sort themselves out.

Autumn came round again and dancing classes commenced at Allington and Marston after the summer break. We also danced once a week at Barford's Social Club to learn the new dances, and social occasions at Croxton and Allington took up our spare time, not to mention the work on the house. In November we cleared the drive of weeds and the all-pervading brambles, mostly by pouring dirty unwanted oil on them and setting fire to it all, drastic but very thorough. Cousin Freda sent us a lot of bulbs and we planted them around the gardens. Bit by bit, inside and out, conditions at the Manor were improving, the hard work put into it had to be seen to be believed.

Croxton church held its annual Christmas Bazaar and made £65 profit. When I stayed at Allington for the weekend I would occasionally go to church there, I found it difficult to get used to such a small building with only one or two bells and, like a lot of churches, not many in the congregation.

Herbert being Baptist, we would sometimes go to the Baptist church in Grantham but I couldn't settle down there, I was too dyed in the wool Anglican, even so I never tried to persuade Herbert to change his religion. His mother was a strong Baptist and had been a lay preacher and Sunday school teacher when living in Liverpool.

Frankie came home to Croxton for his Christmas holiday, still preferring country living and we were all pleased to see him.

Herbert had reared a hundred day-old chicks under a brooder in a hut in the bottom orchard. Now they were grown and ready to be moved to a hut in the paddock, I gave a hand and found myself back to poultry farming.

I spent Christmas at home with my family and Boxing Day at Allington.

On December 28th Croxton was plunged into great sadness, David the son of Cefuss and May Mount was killed whilst helping with the threshing in the farmyard in Chapel Lane, a terrible tragedy.

Herbert and I saw 1951 out on New Year's Eve at the WI party in Allington with the music centre and looked forward to 1952 and our wedding day.

In the New Year Herbert decided he would like a boxer dog, we found that Ganston Kennels bred boxers so taking his mother with us we went to collect one. What an ugly little thing he was, all big eyes, loose skin and snuffly nose. We called him Tango, part of his long pedigree name, and it also tied up with our dancing. He soon grew into a large boisterous dog.

At this time Dad suffered a nasty attack of bronchitis and Mum was having to plod round in the snow and ice with the letters, a difficult job but she seemed to enjoy the winter weather.

Now Herbert was busy getting the kitchen put to rights before our wedding. He scraped the old limewash from the beams and creosoted them, and replastered the walls, Tom lending a hand once or twice. The windows still had original leaded lights, but part had been bricked up because of the window tax, he opened this up and cleaned up the stone mullions, pointed up the new brickwork round the fireplace and soon the place started to look like home.

All this time there were discussions and disagreements about when and where we should be married. We consulted the Rev. Tetley, he said 'no', he couldn't marry us in Croxton Church, the Bishop wouldn't allow it. He did offer us a service of blessing after a registry office wedding. I felt I had to refuse this, as I couldn't see how the Church could refuse to marry us in the sight of God but could give the marriage God's blessing when someone else had tied the knot! We considered the registry office but that put me off altogether. Mum and Dad were disappointed that we thought of having the reception at the Talbot Café in Grantham so we changed the venue to the Stute at Croxton. The Talbot people doing the catering.

Unbeknown to me, Herbert's mother visited the Baptist Minister in Grantham and he invited us to go to see him. He and his wife made us very welcome in their home and after some talking he said he would marry us in his Church in Wharf Road. We chose April 17th for the happy day and felt relieved and thankful that we had found such a sympathetic minister, and that everything was at last settled amicably.

We laid Skinner's bus on to transport guests between Croxton

*Herbert Palin at Grantham*

and the church for the service and back to the reception. Dad wrote out invitations in his distinctive handwriting, all were duly posted and soon replies and presents started to roll in.

Harry Davidson and his Old Tyme Band came to Grantham and we enjoyed an evening of dancing in a large building in Alma Park.

At the end of January there were more hard frosts and snow. The weekend I was staying at the Manor, Mr Jackson had to tow the van out on to the road so that he could take me home.

Sadly on February 6th the nation heard that King George VI had died in his sleep, and the country went into mourning. His daughter Princess Elizabeth and her husband Prince Philip were travelling abroad so it was a sad homecoming for the young Queen of England as she now was. Herbert cancelled his dancing classes and entertainments and all of the country quietened down. The King was buried on February 15th.

At this time Herbert was busy preparing the stands for the Chamber of Trade Exhibition in the Guildhall at Grantham. He was also carving the devil's head to fix on a pair of bellows for his own stand there, thinking that it was appropriate it being the devil's job to keep the fires burning!

The comedians Laurel and Hardy performed the opening ceremony on February 28th. Herbert was photographed at his stand with the Chamber of Trade President, the Secretary, and the Chairman of the Exhibition watching him carve. On the last day of the show Brigadier Grinlin bought the reproduction Gothic table Herbert had made so his first attempt at a show stand proved quite a success.

Whilst he was so busy, I helped organise a dance at Croxton for the Children's Outing Fund and made £15 which we thought was a good profit.

On the day I left Miller's Dental Surgeons, Herbert's Ukrainian friend Alexis Buhryn married Betty Woodward at St Wulfram's church in Grantham and Herbert was best man. They made their home in Alma Park in Grantham.

Herbert and I discussed where to spend our honeymoon, he thinking it would be nice to go over to Holland, but I not liking the idea of the sea journey decided against it. Some friends told him of a grounded aeroplane on the East Coast which had been turned into a holiday home, we felt that this was a better proposition and Herbert booked it for a fortnight from April 17th.

One cold, snowy day Mum, Hetty and myself went to Leicester on the bus to buy our wedding clothes. It was very difficult to know what to choose, a sensible suit or the more traditional dress. In the end I opted for a dress in pale blue lace over taffeta, full length, with a Juliet cap and a short veil. For Hetty almost the same style but in pink with a pink lace, Dutch cap style headdress. We just hoped the cold weather would be gone by April, up to now the early spring weather had been very cold indeed.

Tom started a new job at Barford's factory, he didn't seem to be settling down to civvy life very well at all and had a number of different jobs before returning to his electrical engineering, the trade he had been trained for so long in the army.

Our wedding day was drawing near and the countdown to the great day began. Allington dancing class presented Herbert with an electric wall clock and the Marston class gave a glass dish on a silver stand. On Easter Saturday I scrubbed the house out for Mum, and we decorated the ledge in church and the window, our usual jobs at festivals.

On Easter Sunday Mum and I went to the 9 a.m. Holy Communion Service, which was well attended. Herbert came over in the afternoon and we went for a walk, the weather was beautiful.

On Tuesday we collected the marriage certificate from Melton, and on Wednesday we bought the wedding ring, and a necklace each for Hetty and myself. Later we went down to the Stute to prepare it for the reception, Nurse Bland from Miller's offered to do the flowers for the tables and the Baptist Church, mostly pink and white tulips. Everything looked very nice and ready for the caterers to take over in the morning.

At home Mrs Alexander, the policeman's wife next door, offered me the use of her bathroom instead of my having to use the bath in my bedroom, and all the carrying of water this entailed. I accepted her offer though I wouldn't have minded my last bath at home this way but it was very kind of her to think about it.

To bed at last, all chores done and everything organised for a relaxed start to our big day.

*View from the village of the Old Manor House Allington.*

# 38

# Wedding Day

April 17th dawned bright and warm and everything was set fair for a happy occasion providing I kept my mind away from the church on the hill.

Flowers arrived, my crescent-shaped bouquet of large white tulips, freesias, and hyacinth pips, little bells strung separately on fine wire. Hetty's the same, only pink, to match her dress. Mum's pink carnation corsage and Dad and Tom's carnation buttonholes. Little Andrew Poole came across with a silver horseshoe for 'Good Luck'.

Dad seemed to be bearing up well and I hoped he would keep going, it must have been a strain for him but he insisted on giving me away.

After an early lunch it was time to put on our glad rags. Mum looked very smart and beautiful in her grey moygashell suit, the same style as I had chosen for my going-away outfit, mine being hyacinth blue. Dad in his little-worn navy blue suit, with silver tie, and bowler hat looked no less smart though very frail.

Alone in my bedroom no doubts assailed me, I knew in my heart this was the right thing for both of us. Now dressed in my blue dress and cap I descended the stairs where Mum and Dad were waiting for me in the passage, a poignant moment, after all these years I was leaving their house for the last time in their name.

Hetty arrived looking very attractive, never had a bride such a pretty bridesmaid. Tom who was chauffeuring for the day drove her and Mum off to the Baptist Church in Grantham and Dad and I were alone in the house. It wasn't long before the bridal car arrived and it was our turn to be whisked away. Grandma Poole and Andrew standing on the top of their steps opposite gave us a cheery wave as we drove off. The Baptist Church at last, a crowd had gathered including several Allington people and other people from Croxton we hadn't been able to invite. Photographers were there and after a few minutes posing for them we were walking up the aisle between a church full of friends and well-wishers; I could feel Dad trembling and supported him as best I could hoping that he would manage to get through the service without collapsing. Mr Randall, the dental mechanic from Miller's, played the organ, apparently before I arrived he had made a false start when the nurse from the surgery arrived by playing 'Here comes the Bride'! I'm sure it was a joke by the twinkle in his eye, the crafty old thing, and as I wanted to enter to the first hymn tune 'Praise, my soul, the King of Heaven' it must have been a mistake!

Herbert was waiting at the altar rails with Jim, his best man, his mother saying afterwards that she had never seen him looking so smart. Dad always teased me asking if he would be getting married in his overalls! He *had* been working at Endcliffe Farm in the morning but had found time to change into his wedding attire.

The Minister was very nice and I could feel he was performing the ceremony with great understanding, he made it all very special and I was grateful to him. The service over, the registers were signed and then we were outside in the sunshine receiving 'Good Luck' tokens from small friends. More photographs then we left together as man and wife for the reception at Croxton Stute.

Soon the cars and buses bearing our guests duly arrived and the celebrations were in full swing. Sixty people sat down to cold ham, salads etc. Time to cut the two-tier wedding cake which, strangely enough, had a large sugar model of a church on top, I don't know how that had come about, I hadn't ordered the decoration. The speeches followed, Herbert's mother and Uncle Sam had their say and Jim took the stand, all their sentiments being 'we were well suited', their advice 'to make sure there was plenty of give and take in our lives together', then they were sure we would make a success of our marriage! Jim opened thirteen telegrams from people who hadn't been able to be with us. This part of the proceedings over, the tables were pushed back and the dancing began, old tyme of course, what else for us and our old tyme contempories.

At last it was back to Middle Street to change into our going-away clothes and to say goodbye to Dad who had retired there immediately after the speeches. He was tired but had stood up to all the excitement very well indeed.

Even Mum hadn't thought Herbert's little Bubby Hutch a suitable chariot to carry away a bride so he had discreetly left it parked outside Jim's shop in Finkin Street, Tom was to drive us into town to pick it up from there.

We had a great send-off from the Stute and we were on our way at last, Tom giving us a hairy ride into Grantham and seeing us safely transferred to our little van crammed to the roof with everything needed for our honeymoon. We had been later leaving Croxton than we had anticipated and dusk had set in as we neared Skegness and our destination Trunch Lane Caravan Site. We lost our way in the narrow coastal lanes and it was quite dark by the time we arrived at our G-Avro aeroplane. We found everything to our liking, the body of the plane was large, the wings and nose being removed, windows and glass doors had been inserted to form an entrance lobby and a sun porch, through to the large living/sleeping area, with a narrow passage at the rear to a washroom, toilet and small kitchen. It was tucked away in the corner of a small site, empty now except for one or two people there for the Easter weekend. The weather was very good most of the time and we were able to sun-bathe in the sand dunes. We went to the cinema at Skegness to see *Where no Vultures Fly* and on Sunday we went to Addlethorpe church where many years later Herbert was to restore the chancel screen. Herbert made a start on painting my portrait in oils and the days quickly passed.

We had so enjoyed our little home by the sea but the end of the honeymoon was in sight, we had to think about getting back into the real world and to a new life together at the Old Manor House in Allington.

*Our Wedding Day, 17th April 1952.*

We left Tudor II, as the aeroplane was called, swept and tidied, ash trays emptied of the assortment of objects acquired during the last happy days. Small pots of cowslips and palm were thrown out, the curtains primly drawn and bedding stowed away, the kitchen washed down and everything in its place, the washroom neat and empty with only the lingering smell of shaving soap to betray the recent occupants. The coat hangers naked on their rods behind the flowered curtains, and here and there bits of bright confetti lay persistently clinging to the blue carpet as reluctant as we to leave the honeymoon home.

At last, our baggage stowed away in the van, the portrait resting proudly on top we left to the music of the host of larks singing in the glorious blue of an April sky and the distant swishing of the sea beyond the sand hills.

# 39

# Settling In

We arrived home at the Manor late in the afternoon to find Mother Palin busy in the kitchen making what she called balm cakes. Actually they were small bread cobs, very tasty and, try as I might, I could never make them like she could. She always said she used the same ingredients as I did, but they tasted so much better than mine, I used to think she used a secret ingredient she wasn't letting on about.

Nothing seemed to be mine, it took a very long time for it to really feel like home to me.

The next few days were spent settling in, going over to Croxton to pack up wedding presents and cut up the cake and send it off to those friends who hadn't been able to get to the wedding. Several new presents had arrived and were laid out with the others in the parlour. We saved the top tier of the cake hopefully for the christening of our first baby, carefully wrapping it up and placing it in an airtight tin, never doubting that it would keep well until our firstborn arrived.

Food was still rationed so I had to get a new ration book, and change my name on bank books etc. Mother Palin was registered with Rowell's, the grocers in Vine Street in Grantham, the village shop not stocking rationed food. I hadn't had much dealings with rations so had to learn fast how to make a little go a long way.

The big job in the house was to get the kitchen finished off, the ceiling was scraped clean of the old whitewash and the beams creosoted. Herbert limewashed the wall and soon all was fresh and white. The floor, half flagstones and half old red brick, had to stay like that for a long time to come. We filled the large Welsh dresser with blue and white Cornish ware and willow pattern dishes, laid a rug in front of the small iron stove and things began to look like home. Mother Palin went to Liverpool to stay with Aunt Dolly, her friend and a surrogate aunt, and for a while we had the house to ourselves.

In the workshop Herbert was busy making a show stand for Swallow's, the corn merchants in Grantham. This kept him busy all hours but at last it was finished and taken to Belton House to be erected in the grounds for the Lincolnshire Agricultural Show. Alas, no sooner was it made ready when a terrific thunderstorm broke overhead and the roof was damaged, more panic to get it right again and all was well. Herbert and I visited the show on the second day and found that the stand had won First Prize for the best stand on the show ground, we had lunch there with light hearts.

Herbert was commissioned to carve a trophy for the Camera Club. He designed a naked lady sitting inside a camera reflector. It was accepted and was soon executed and on show in the window of Walter Lee's photography studio on the High Street.

Summer was moving on apace and almost every Saturday was taken up by going to garden fetes in the surrounding villages with the music and amplifiers.

The soft fruit bushes in the garden yielded good crops of currants, gooseberries and raspberries, so I was kept busy making jams and bottling lots of them in good old Kilner jars. The years spent at Croxton Lodge standing me in good stead for making the most of the fruit harvest, and the old dairy shelves filled up with preserves for the winter months.

In July Uncle Bert and Auntie Bea from Canada came to stay with us bringing with them groceries and much soap and soap powder, evidently thinking that we were starving and possibly in need of a good wash! Uncle Bert was Mother Palin's brother who had gone over to Canada before the First World War with only the proverbial sixpence in his pocket. He went into the haulage business there and prospered. Now he was managing a fish hatchery in North Bay, and had a grown up family of three, Helen, Shirley and Howard.

At this time Herbert came across a chap with a large swarm of bees in his garden in Grantham who did not know what to do about it. We had heard of Mrs Stubley at Belvoir, a great authority on these matters and locally called the 'Queen Bee', so Herbert contacted her and she went over and took the swarm, much to her delight and gratitude and the man's relief. Later to show her appreciation she invited us to tea with her in her cosy flat over the stables of Belvoir, quite an experience.

Mr Ballard, the farmer at Endcliffe Farm along Bottesford Lane, was short of helpers for his harvest so appealed to Herbert and he found himself working long hours in the harvest fields.

The pullets were laying well and we were able to sell some eggs at the door, as well as let the egg man take a dozen or two each week.

Dr. Woll, our local doctor at Bottesford, asked us if we would consider letting her rent a room to hold a surgery in Allington. We decided to let her have the butler's pantry, at the foot of the main staircase. Not having got round to restoring it, we had to set to and clear out all the years of junk and cobwebs. We opened up the bricked-up windows, scraped walls and ceilings and replastered. Glass had been hard to come by after the war so Herbert had bought up a lot of old pictures from the market and made do with the glass. There were worn steps going down into the cellar from this room with a very nice turned-oak balustrade at the top, Herbert stripped these and polished them, but the steps had to be boarded over for safety. The exposed timbers in the walls were creosoted and the wall decorated in a very pretty green, furniture was installed and, after weeks of hard work, in November the room was ready to receive its first Allington patients, Dr Woll paying us £10 a year for the privilege.

Sometimes Aunt and Uncle took Mother Palin away with them on their sightseeing trips and then Mother and Frankie would visit us, Frankie giving us a good hand with mowing down the ever-present nettles and thistles and cleaning out chicken huts, which was a great help. Aunt and Uncle sailed for Canada and home on Uncle's birthday, October 16th, on RMS *Franconia*, Mother Palin going to Liverpool to see them off.

Mrs Shipman wrote to me for my birthday telling me that Bill and Frankie's brother John and a gang of women were busy picking up the potatoes, a good crop of ten tons to the acre. Molly was busy blood testing her hens, a job I had often helped her with.

At a meeting of the members of the Coronation Entertainment Committee held at the Manor we planned to start a Coronation fund with donations from the village. Later we held socials and other events to raise money for the celebration on Coronation Day.

We started the dancing classes again at Allington and Marston and went one night a week to Barford's Social Club to learn new dances.

Herbert was helping Mr Ballard with his threshing and in the workshop he was making a shooting brake for John Cocksworth.

Grantham Drama Society were putting on a show called *Miranda* for which Herbert set up the music centre.

Life was getting very hectic and our first winter together was almost upon us.

In the dining room there was an odd sort of corner, a doorway which opened almost directly on to an outside wall in which there was a bricked-up window, however if one looked to the left there was a low opening leading into the cubby hole under the back stairs. On the opposite wall there was a low bricked-up doorway, which would have led into the kitchen and so out through the back door. This led us to believe it was a priest's bolthole.

However, the various architects and historians who visited us didn't go along with this idea but we stuck with it because we liked to think so! Herbert opened up the window which looked out into the drive and reglazed it. He replastered the walls and hung the door so that we could have it open during the day and closed at night to keep out the draughts and the cats who weren't too particular about using the corner as a loo when no one was looking!

Snow fell in November and sought out the nooks and crannies under the roof tiles and other weak spots of the building and drifted in wherever it could. Herbert had to go up on the roof in the valley between the two roofs and shovel it off to avert further disaster. Buckets were placed at strategic points to catch the drips and towels laid along the back windowsills to mop up the melted snow.

We held the Coronation Social in the village hall and £4. 2s. 6d. was added to the £28 already in the kitty.

Christmas was approaching, Mum gave me fruit to make her Christmas cake along with my own, alas they were a failure, I wasn't yet too good at baking with electricity. Had to make two more which, thankfully, weren't too bad!

The Rev. Spreadbury asked me if I would be treasurer for the church's Christmas Bazaar, I agreed but hoped I wouldn't get things too muddled up, monetary affairs not being my forte! It was held on December 6th and we made over £50 profit which I handed over to Mr Polfreman, the churchwarden.

We decided to go round carol singing to swell the funds of the Coronation appeal. Mr Kirk from the old camp along the Sedgebrook road brought his organ up to the Manor and practices took place in the dilapidated hall.

In the meantime various friends were making their first visits to the Manor and Christmas shopping had to be done. Sweets were still on coupons and food continued to be rationed, though we were allowed double rations for Christmas. Our wireless was in need of a new valve so Mother Palin gave us one for Christmas.

The weather was snowy and our little van temperamental, Bert Jackson having to give Herbert a tow out on to the road more than once to get it started.

We were trying to get the house in some sort of order in time for Christmas. Herbert swept the dining room chimney and I put in a lot of elbow grease on the floors, and staircases, to settle the everlasting dust and dirt, which covered everything.

On Christmas Eve I cleaned the kitchen then had to catch the bus into

Grantham to meet Frankie and do some shopping for Mum. Herbert met me there then we had to go to Harlaxton pub to fix up the music centre for their evening's entertainment. We spent so much time there we were late getting home and found the carol singers all waiting for us at the house ready to start on their rounds. Herbert had to have a quick snack and they were off on their ways, I stayed behind to see Mother Palin off to bed and feed the cats and dogs, Mrs Columbel, a farmer's wife from the village, staying with me. We caught the singers up outside the Welby Arms after they had been along Bottesford Lane. Then round the side streets to where Mrs Burton was waiting for us at her house with coffee and mince pies, which was greatly appreciated, it certainly helped us on our chilly way. We finished up at the camp and on counting up the money at Mr Kirk's house found that we had made £4. On the whole a successful venture and a lot of people seemed to appreciate our efforts.

Christmas Day was spent between home and Croxton, going there after dinner. Mum seemed very tired and unwell after her Christmas mail deliveries, but had done very well for Christmas boxes.

We relaxed at home on Boxing Day. Mum and Frankie, Tom and Phyllis coming to tea the next day and going home on the 9.20 p.m. bus.

Jim and Kitty, his wife, were living over their shop in Finkin Street, Grantham. On the Sunday after Christmas Herbert, Mother Palin and myself went to dinner with them.

On New Year's Eve we went over to Croxton to see if anyone had duck eggs for sale, we fancied putting some under a broody hen, but weren't lucky in this respect, no one had ducks let alone their eggs! Home again and after a few household chores we saw the New Year in, Herbert going out of the back door and I letting him in through the front bringing in a lump of coal.

We toasted 1953 in with a glass of Mother Palin's ginger wine.

# 40

## 1953

We started the New Year off with a small party, Mother Palin, Jim and Kitty, and Eric and Elvie Wheeler, Elvie being the headmistress of Croxton School. Then it was back to normal.

Herbert grained the doors in the Doctor's room. Tom came over and fixed the light over the village hall door. Jim's café and music shop was now fully in business in the Market Place in Grantham.

Frankie had left school now and was back in Croxton, living with Mum and Dad permanently and working at Croxton Lodge farm. During this time he was confirmed into the Church of England.

We had another social for the Coronation fund, many people offering their talents in support. Friends came over from Marston to put on a little play, a friend Paddy danced an Irish jig, Mrs Thurlby from Croxton sang her favourite songs 'Danny Boy' and 'The Lost Chord'. All this with dancing, games and refreshments made an enjoyable evening, our profits being £4. Gradually our fund was growing.

Towards the end of January we were all shocked by the terrible floods which devastated the East Coast. High winds and tides breached the sea defences and swept away houses and lives were lost. Police and rescue workers were called to the coast from all parts of Lincolnshire. Later in February we organised a dance in aid of flood relief.

Another social was held for the Coronation fund, considering Allington was such a small place then, we seemed to be asking for a lot of money but people on the whole supported everything very well.

Our own private lives were gathering speed, Herbert was getting busier in the workshop, and trying to keep up with the house restoration, keeping the vegetable gardens in order and seeing to the poultry. Inside I was battling with dust and housekeeping. Our main task now being to make a small flat up the back stairs for Mother Palin.

Herbert took out the old stone surround from the open fireplace in one of the bedrooms, and slid the great stones down the back stairs to the hall where he fitted them into the gaping hole in the end wall where there had obviously been a fireplace. They fitted so perfectly that he concluded that they had originally come from that particular place.

When Herbert had first started on the restoration there had been another fireplace in the opposite wall but he had taken this out and fitted it into the dining room, bricking up the hole he had left. Now there was just one fireplace with its beautifully moulded stone surround. He set a small Edwardian fireplace into the bedroom and put up a wooden mantelpiece and surround, much more suitable for the small room. Opening up windows, replacing and rebuilding faulty brickwork all took a vast amount of time but eventually it was all finished and decorated and it became the sitting room to the 'Flat'. Leading off from this room was a small walk-in cupboard or passage with a connecting door to the next bedroom alongside the large kitchen chimneybreast. Herbert fastened up the end door and fixed a small sink in the window alcove, brought the water through from the bathroom and there was a small kitchenette.

The room opposite this room and at the foot of more stairs leading up to the roof was the next thing to tackle. Here all the same procedures had to be followed, windows opened up, replastering etc. There was already a small 'ducks nest' fireplace here and the floor was made of very wide boards, the only wooden floor upstairs the others being Lincolnshire plaster. This room was soon made ready and became the bedroom to the flat, and Mother Palin moved into her own private quarters.

In April I was to receive a letter from the Rev. Spreadbury asking if I would consider taking on the job of rector's warden at Allington church. Thinking it over I decided the time wasn't quite right, I was only a newcomer, and I wondered if he knew we had been refused permission to marry in the Anglican Church. He said he did know and felt that had been most unfortunate and didn't make any difference in his attitude towards me.

On April 18th Tom married his fiancée, Phyllis, at St Anne's church, Grantham, with a small reception afterwards at Phyllis's parents' home in Dudley Road. They went away to Keswick in the Lake District for their honeymoon, coming back again to live in two rooms there until they could manage to get a house of their own.

Neville Read, who had been doing odd jobs about the place whilst still at school, started his full-time apprenticeship in the workshop with Herbert.

We were still carrying on with meetings and fund raising for the Coronation celebrations. Meals were planned for the day for the whole village and mugs were purchased for the children, and at last the great day arrived.

Disappointingly on June 6th, the Coronation Day, it poured with rain and our proud flags and bunting hung sad and limp. Meals had to be held in the village hall, but it was a happy occasion nevertheless.

Queen Elizabeth II was now our crowned queen, the pomp and splendour of her Coronation in Westminster Abbey was the first royal occasion to be televised.

That year Herbert and Neville attended the Lincolnshire Show at Brigg being part of the Rural Industries stand with other craftsmen and women.

In August Dr. Woll confirmed that I was pregnant, we were delighted and set about restoring another room for the nursery. Again an end window was opened up, this one in the long narrow room next to the bathroom, and the walls restored and replastered.

At last Herbert papered it in a light background paper with large panels of nursery rhyme paper over it. Alas, after a few weeks all the paper started to crack off, dry and brittle. We had to think that we hadn't prepared the wall underneath properly, the size used not compatible with the old limewash or whatever had been used on the walls in past times. We had to clean it all down again, we repapered it this time in a pretty floral pattern and all was well.

So our second summer was passing swiftly, I kept very well except for ankle trouble which resulted me in seeing an orthopaedic specialist in Grantham Hospital. After X-rays he told me there wasn't much he could do and he thought it would improve after baby was born.

Tom and Phyllis's baby was born on August 17th, the same day as Gran Palin's birthday.

In November Dad was ill again and confined to bed, he didn't seem to make any progress. The doctor promised to get him into Grantham Hospital, but the appointment never came. Finally his condition worsened and he was admitted, after a few days there Mum was sent for, Mr Poole taking her there one morning. Mrs Selby brought a message to me at the Manor saying Dad was worse and to go to the hospital immediately. Herbert was out on a job, I hurried across to the Jacksons to see if they could give me a lift there but their car was out. Mrs Jackson rang Mr Palfreyman and he obliged immediately and I was at the hospital in record time. I was sent to the waiting room where later Herbert joined me and we expected to see Mum. No sign of her, in fact nobody about at all, the place seemed deserted. At last Sister appeared and said, "Would you like to see your father now?" "Of course we would," we said. She looked strangely at us and I suddenly realized that Dad was already dead. Very shocked I asked where my mother was. "She's gone, I'm afraid," was the reply.

Poor Mum hadn't got to the hospital in time to see Dad before he died and had now gone off to find Tom and Phyllis in Dudley Road. Tom had not managed to get to the hospital as he was working out of town and had no transport so it had been a mix-up all round. We visited the side ward where Dad was still propped up on his pillows, peaceful at last, then off we went to find Mum. She was just coming out of the Dale's house with Tom and Phyllis to go and catch the bus home to Croxton, so brave and independent. From there we took over and looked after her, staying at Croxton until after the funeral.

Once again the slow procession up to church, many friends joining us in our sorrow. Someone had produced a Union Jack which draped the coffin and Dad was buried in the family plot slightly behind Maisie and Grandad by the north-east corner of the church by the vestry window. Mum wouldn't come back to Allington with us, "No thank you," she said, "I've got to get used to being on my own now." She spent Christmas with us but it was a sad time. We looked forward to a happier 1954 and the birth of our eagerly awaited baby.

Early in January 1954 violent gales and storms created havoc all over our country and breakdowns in the electricity supply. We were using candles to light us on our way, going to bed by candle-light in the old house seemed a step back in history.

Herbert was working on John Cocksworth's shop fittings in Grantham. At this time he thought he would like to join the Red Rose Guild of Craftsmen and applied for membership. We had to make a trip up to Manchester to the Whitworth Art Galleries with a sample of his work. The night before we set off I packed up a box of food to take to Aunt Annie, Mother Palin's sister, with whom we were to stay for the few days we were there. Apples, eggs, butter, crab apple jelly and a couple of rabbits were included.

Next morning gave promise of a fine windy day, but by the time we reached the other side of Nottingham the rain started and never stopped all the way to Manchester. Crossing the moors the wind thundered at us and the rain swept across the hills in great solid sheets. Swollen streams rushed and tumbled everywhere, but our brave little van carried us on through wind and water and we arrived at Hyde Road just as Uncle Joe was going upstairs for his afternoon nap. That evening we went to see Herbert's cousin Annie and Jim, her husband, at their house in Denton.

The next morning we took examples of Herbert's work to the Whitworth Art Galleries to be assessed by the powers that be as to whether Herbert was skilful enough to be admitted to the Red Rose Guild of Craftsmen. On collecting the pieces later in the day we were disappointed to learn that he had not been accepted as a member, perhaps later he could try again. We visited another cousin, Emmie, and her husband in the evening, like us they were expecting a baby in April.

Next day we returned home, calling on my old ATS friend Mary in Rochdale. Her mother gave us lunch after which Mary took us over to her twin's school to meet them both, charming little girls and very much like their Canadian father. Sadly Mary and he were now separated and living apart, one of the Canadian war brides whose marriage didn't work out. Fog had closed in as we made our way home and blocked out the beautiful landscape I had hoped to see on our way back. We arrived safely in Nottingham and had a meal there reaching home late evening tired and disappointed at the outcome of our trip.

Next morning I felt tired and not at all cheered by the knowledge that we now had an overdraft of £58.

Neville had managed very well whilst we had been away, even washing the weekly egg supply ready for the egg man. The pullets were laying well and some weeks we had as many as 20 dozen, the present price being 4s. 3½d. a dozen.

Tom was still talking of getting a house, his little family still living in the Dale's house in Dudley Road, but he didn't seem to be getting very far in his search for one.

Mum was beginning to brighten up a bit and thinking of getting back to her posting round. Meeting her in town one day for her eye test I learned that Flook, Frankie's little black dog, had had to be shot for chasing sheep. Apparently it and an alsatian belonging to the school teacher had been caught in the act, and the farmer had insisted Flook paid the price, the alsatian getting off scot-free, I never could understand that. Mum and Frankie were heartbroken, Flook had been such a comfort to them since Dad died.

Frankie had another disappointment that week too, a letter from his Mother told him that his sister Lily had got married, he had been hoping for an invitation to the wedding.

I felt very depressed about the loss of Dad and Flook, but the baby was kicking around like mad so it didn't seem as though the long journey to Manchester had harmed it.

I went to Croxton to collect an old wicker dress basket which I was going to make into a first crib. Herbert collected me on his way home from modelling class in Grantham where he was making a model of Tango.

He had grown into a large lolloping energetic dog, jumping around like an overgrown puppy, worrying me a bit when he landed not too gently on my expanding tummy.

Worried about money matters we approached the bank to see about mortgaging the house, but they said they didn't arrange mortgages but would help us temporarily. Herbert was now working in town doing the fittings in the laboratory at Swallow's, the corn merchants. Sometimes I would meet him after work and we would have tea at Jim's Café and an evening at the pictures.

The weather turned bitterly cold and the water tank in the roof froze and the wireless licence reminder came through the door with the mail! It snowed and Mum and Frankie came for a visit.

Tom had applied for a job with GEC in Coventry and went to live in digs there for a while. He didn't stay long as he and Phyllis didn't like living apart and he was soon home again. Still it snowed, Herbert having to go round upstairs to see exactly where the pipes had frozen with a blow lamp. I bought three yards of peach art silk from Grantham and lined the dress basket and made a little quilted eiderdown to match. On the outside of the basket I fixed an old, cream bed valence, Herbert made a stand for it and, hey presto, the sweetest little crib you ever saw. I busily knitted vests and matinee jackets, Mrs Cox from Croxton sent two little jackets and two pairs of booties, very kind of her.

Snow disappeared but frost and fog continued, and so did the battle with the frozen pipes. Standing at the kitchen sink was like standing outside, the windows as yet not very weather proof.

In February Aunt and Uncle in Canada let us know that they would be visiting us again in May. Jim was still dodging backwards and forwards to Devon, setting up a wool shop in Dartmouth.

The district nurse was visiting me at intervals keeping her eye on baby's progress, giving me a form to fill in for my maternity benefit.

The Wheelers left the School House in Croxton and Eric had taken a job as farm manager in Honeybourne near Broughton on the Water.

I decided I had better do a bit of spring cleaning, as much as one could do under the dusty circumstances that still prevailed in a good bit of the house. Herbert swept the dining room chimney and I scrubbed and cleaned, Mum coming over at the weekend to give a hand with washing up and egg washing etc., a great help. She would then go home on the 9.20 p.m. bus from Allington getting a connection easily out to Croxton.

The doctor disappointed me one morning by saying she would like a second opinion on my ankles, and warned me if I didn't rest more I would have to have the baby in hospital. I had been looking forward to a home confinement, fancying to have our first baby actually born at the Manor and I hoped and prayed it would be so.

Tango disappeared, Herbert went looking all over for him but no sign of him anywhere. The baker told us that one of his customers had seen two men in a red van playing with a dog, when they went away they took the dog with them. We went to the police station in Gonerby to report this information and the sergeant said he would check on it. Later he let us know that a farm worker had had to pull a van out of a ditch along Bottesford Lane with his tractor, he had seen Tango and had questioned the men, they told him that they had sold us some lino and instead of money had paid for it with the dog! It had never occurred to him that the dog was stolen. After a day or two Mr Ballard, the farmer along the lane, let us know that he had seen a dog like Tango jump out of a van in Radcliffe on Trent. That sounded hopeful, perhaps he would find his way home after all. We visited the lost dogs' home at Radcliffe but he hadn't been handed in. The police said the lino men were from Sheffield so we hadn't much hope of seeing Tango again, nor did we ever find him.

Snow was falling again and sharp frost persisted, our journeys visiting Mum at Croxton were tricky indeed through the frost bound lanes.

In the meantime I was busy assembling the layette and, when the sun shone, washing the bundles of new nappies: butter muslin for next to the skin and terry towelling ones over the top.

Big snowdrifts blocked the roads and made travelling difficult. Phyllis told us of another baby on the way, and Tom couldn't find them anywhere to live in Coventry.

We finally put a notice in the Grantham Journal asking if anyone had seen Tango but we received no replies so we had to accept the fact that he had gone forever.

New council houses in Harlem's Field at Croxton were being allocated. One or two young couples from Croxton and one or two strangers were the lucky tenants, we had hoped that Tom would get one. Perhaps he would stand a chance later, he wasn't too keen on being a council tenant, but 'needs must when the devil drives'.

The doctor was still saying that I might not have to go into hospital for my confinement but I wasn't so sure and took each day as it came.

Herbert was working on the end bedroom hoping to get it done before the baby was born. Busy days followed busy days and I tried to rest as much as I could but it wasn't easy. Resting on the bed one day Herbert was showing an architect round the house, he opened the bedroom door with a flourish and there I was reclining on the bed like a stranded whale! Another afternoon I was relaxing on the bed when Gran Palin roused me saying there was a sow and piglets in the garden rooting up the veggies etc., oughtn't I to go and drive them out? I wasn't too keen on going but felt I couldn't let the garden be devastated. The chicken meal arrived from Silcock's and oak from Coultas's and as Herbert was away working I had to cope, and so the struggle went on. I cashed my maternity cheque for £9 and did the final bits of baby shopping.

Tom's daughter Theresa was christened at St John's church, Grantham on March 14th, I being one of the Godmothers. She was a good girl, didn't cry at all, according to the old folk she would have done to 'let the devil out'. Come the spring of 1954, Jim and Kitty were not yet settled in Dartmouth, Kitty still living in Grantham.

Snowdrops covered the front garden and miniature daffodils appeared in the grass around the base of the trees. Later followed by a great bed of stars of Bethlehem and then larger daffodils appeared, new life bursting everywhere.

As time went by the doctor got more and more worried about my condition and sent me off to Peel St. Hospital in Nottingham. There the consultant said she wanted to admit me right away, but I couldn't stay then, as there were things to be arranged at home. Herbert drove me there the next day and I was admitted. The doctor, on her rounds the day after, was upset because my blood pressure was as high as ever, rather crossly she said if I didn't settle down she would move me to where I wouldn't be able to see anything or talk to anyone. She 'hoped I was taking my tablets properly', I was mystified by that, I told her I hadn't been given any sort of medicine since arriving there. Great panic and consternation and a reprimand for the persons responsible and tablets were quickly given.

So the slow days passed. The large ward filled with heavily pregnant women with their own hair-raising tales to tell, not very encouraging to someone about to have their first baby.

After the first week I felt a twinge of pain and was whisked off to the delivery room and they telephoned Herbert to tell him not to come till the next day. They tried to administer a general anaesthetic but I didn't seem to take it very well and drifted off into oblivion. The last thing I heard as I struggled to take in the gas was the anaesthetist saying, "Good heavens this girl has more gas in her than half a dozen bar maids." I woke up to find myself still in the delivery room and a kindly nurse bending over me, I could hear little murmurings in the corner of the room, "You have a little girl," she said. She fetched the baby to me and put her in my arms and we were both trundled off via long corridors and lifts back to the general ward. 'Thought you'd gone for good' was the greeting I got from the others, all agog to know how I got on. It appeared that I had many stitches inside and out and found sitting up very painful, otherwise I wasn't feeling too bad. The baby had been taken away to the nursery and I didn't see her again till the next day.

Herbert visited us in the afternoon and he went to see her, thrilled to bits with his new offspring, who by now we had decided to call Nanette Jane. My mother's name had been Annie but she was called Nan so we thought 'little Nan' was appropriate, Jane was Herbert's mother's name, so we pleased them both. After visiting time in the afternoon Herbert

*Nanette with.Mummy.*

went off to have his tea somewhere, intending to visit again in the evening, but 'Dads' piled into the ward and no Herbert, I wondered where he had got to, and thought he had maybe decided to go home to Allington after all. Come the end of visiting time and footsteps pounded along the corridor it was 'Daddy', he had gone to the cinema to pass the time and when he came out couldn't remember where he had parked the car and had spent an hour searching for it. We didn't have many minutes together then, but he visited most afternoons, and Mum and friends did manage to get over to see us. I was moved to a single room in another part of the hospital and had to stay there another two weeks until my stitches were taken out. It would be nice to say I enjoyed my time in hospital but it wasn't a very happy time, but having our beautiful daughter made up for other deficiencies. At last the day came when we were allowed to go home. Mrs Ballard insisted that we let her husband fetch us out, as our little van wasn't draughtproof enough to bring our baby home to the Manor. Theirs was a super car, comfortable and warm and she had given him instructions that we three were to be allowed to sit in the back, a little family to ourselves, we did appreciate it.

Gran Palin was waiting at the front door to welcome us and Herbert handed over our little bundle to her and her joy knew no bounds. She and Herbert took Nanette upstairs to her sitting room where I joined them after thanking Mr Ballard for his kindness and he assuring himself that I was happy.

Mrs Ulliot, who cleaned at the Old Manor House, had a sister who had come from Sheffield to help me during my first week at home and I was

*August 1954. Nanette with Auntie Bea*

*The Old Manor House, Allington.*

glad of her, as I was very stiff and weaker than I expected to be. As the days went by I gained strength and was soon back to normal, Nanette thriving all the time.

Mum received notice that the Duke of Rutland was about to sell off some of the houses in Croxton allowing the tenants to buy them for a reasonable amount of money. The house had been occupied by Mum's family before her, and her grandparents before that, so she was able to buy it for £150 which after some thought, she decided to do. Some of the smaller cottages went for £50 or £60. Ted Creasey, now out of the Navy and working as a solicitor's clerk in Melton, was a great help negotiating a mortgage for them and managing the other business pertaining to buying a house.

*Nanette Jane Palin, one year old with Gran Palin.*

Dr. Woll and Dr Spalding continued to use the doctor's room as their branch surgery once a week and I dished out the prescriptions for their patients.

The Rev. Spreadbury kept his eye on us, delighting in the fact that there was a pram standing in the Manor's garden after years of emptiness and neglect. He christened Nanette Jane in Holy Trinity church on May 23rd, Jean Creasey and Hetty Scott being her godmothers and Uncle Tom her godfather. Gran Palin was away staying with Jim and Kitty and didn't come for the christening.

Uncle Bert and Aunt Bea visited us again from Canada in May and stayed until September. On Septmber 26th Gran Palin received a letter from them to say they had arrived safely at Pine Croft, Aunt Annie's home, they were to stay there for a week before resuming their journey to North Bay. They had carried with them a cast iron plaque, which they had acquired from Dorrington Station with Herbert's great-uncle John Williams' name on it below the notice 'To whom it may concern'. Christmas again and Nanette's first, Father Christmas visited and we felt sure he would find the wide chimneys of the Old Manor House much to his liking!